ISO 9000
Management Systems
Manual

Other ISO Books of Interest

ISO 9000 Management Systems Manual

James S. Davies

McGraw-Hill

New York   San Francisco   Washington, D.C.   Auckland   Bogotá
Caracas   Lisbon   London   Madrid   Mexico City   Milan
Montreal   New Delhi   San Juan   Singapore
Sydney   Tokyo   Toronto

Library of Congress Cataloging-in-Publication Data
Davies, James S.
   ISO 9000 management systems manual / James S. Davies.
     p. cm.
   Includes index.
   ISBN 0-07-015768-5
   1. ISO 9000 Series Standards—Handbooks, manuals, etc.
  2. Industrial management—Handbooks, manuals, etc. I. Title.
   TS156.6.D38   1996
   658.5′62—dc21   96-48236
                                                   CIP

McGraw-Hill

*A Division of The **McGraw·Hill** Companies*

1 2 3 4 5 6 7 8 9 0 KGP / KGP 9 0 2 1 0 9 8 7

ISBN 0-07-015768-5

The sponsoring editor for this book was Harold B. Crawford, the editing supervisor was Fred Dahl, and the production supervisor was Pamela A. Pelton. It was set in Baskerville by Inkwell Publishing Services.

Printed and bound by Quebecor.

The text from ANSI/ASQC Q9001 (1994) appears with the kind permission of the American Society For Quality Control (ASQC), 611 East Windsor Ave., PO Box 3005, Milwaukee, WI 53201. Copyright © 1994, ASQC. The figures from BS 4891 and BS 6143 appear with the kind permission of the British Standards Institution (BSI), Linford Wood West, Milton Keynes. MK14 6LL. United Kingdom. Copyright © 1972, 1990, BSI.

This book is printed on acid-free paper.

McGraw-Hill books are available at special quantity discounts to use as premiums and sales promotions, or for use in corporate training programs. For more information, please write to the Director of Special Sales, McGraw-Hill, 11 West 19th Street, New York, NY 10011. Or contact your local bookstore.

Quick Reference Guide

Quick Reference Guide

Quick Reference Guide

Section	Factsheet Title	Description	Ref. #
Management	Quality Policy	ISO 9001 Clause 4.1.1	136
	Organization	ISO 9001 Clause 4.1.2	138
	Management Representative	ISO 9001 Clause 4.1.2.3	140
	Quality Planning	ISO 9001 Clause 4.2.3	142
	Management Review	ISO 9001 Clause 4.1.3	144
	Exercises	Tutorial on Management elements of ISO 9001	147
Continuous Improvement	Corrective and Preventive Action	ISO 9001 Clause 4.14	154
	Internal Quality Audits	ISO 9001 Clause 4.17	159
	Control of Nonconforming Product	ISO 9001 Clause 4.13	163
	Statistical Techniques	ISO 9001 Clause 4.20	165
	Exercises	Tutorial on Continuous Improvement elements of ISO 9001	167
Product/ Service Lifecycle	Contract Review	ISO 9001 Clause 4.3	172
	Design Control	ISO 9001 Clause 4.4	174
	Process Control	ISO 9001 Clause 4.9	179
	Handling, Storage, etc.	ISO 9001 Clause 4.15	181
	Servicing	ISO 9001 Clause 4.19	183
	Exercises	Tutorial on Lifecycle elements of ISO 9001	184

Quick Reference Guide

I commend each and every author who has managed to complete a book. Although ultimately satisfying, it is one of the most painful processes a person can endure. Speaking of processes, the process inputs in this instance were factsheets that I used to stimulate discussion in workgroups with clients. What evolved by way of output was a documented methodology representing an effective ISO 9000 implementation approach. Hopefully it will prove as valuable to you as it has to me.

These are interesting times for industry at large. Markets are constantly evolving, forcing companies themselves to undergo rapid and far-reaching changes. Massive advances in technology, a better educated consumer, globalization of markets, repositioning, diversification.... companies these days simply cannot afford to rely on the ways of the past. But such change, albeit necessary, has proved to be painful and costly if not supported by the necessary management systems and controls.

Depending on which management or quality authority you subscribe to, or what articles you've read recently, companies are looking for the solution to this change from a variety of sources: process improvement exercises, total quality management, business process reengineering, ISO 9000, to name but a few. When companies have embraced the need for change, it then becomes a question of how best to support, manage, and control that organizational change (and the cultural shift it requires).

This Manual considers change from one particular angle: structured and controlled change based on the disciplines and strengths associated with building an effective quality management system. More specifically it explores the role of an integrated system supporting process, quality, and business management around a core infrastructure proposed by the ISO 9000 series of standards. Such a system is referred to as a *Business Management System.*

The Business Management System (BMS) represents the logical evolution of a quality management system. Gone are the days of quality manuals that map directly to the text and structure of what is, after all, an unfriendly standard. Industry has matured enough to realize that business management and quality management are in fact one and the same. As witnessed in the global explosion of ISO 9000, industry is also now beginning to see the real strength of ISO 9000: the framework it provides for effective enterprise-wide management.

It is difficult to ignore the impact of ISO 9000. Over two decades, the international momentum behind ISO 9000 (and its predecessor, BS 5750) has steadily grown to the point that it is becoming a requirement for doing business. While an estimated 100,000 or more companies worldwide have achieved compliance to ISO 9000, only a number of these companies have truly realized the full potential of ISO 9000 and its framework for a Business Management System.

Unfortunately ISO 9000 is still recognized more for its marketing edge than its role as a powerful management tool. Although ISO 9000 compliance is addressed throughout the Manual, the focus is more in the areas of process management and continuous process improvement.

Preface

There is no shortage of books on ISO 9000 or quality in the market. In fact, the number of reference books is beginning to display a similar growth curve to the number of ISO 9000 registrations worldwide! Once you have started to use this Manual, however, I hope that you will agree that it is different from most others in a number of ways.

The Manual includes integrated factsheets that address the role of quality management, ISO 9000, quality management projects, and management system design. These factsheets are built around a methodology that will take an organization from early quality management awareness toward quality system maturity and world-class practices. To be as practical as possible, it was designed as a user-friendly toolkit of materials, concepts, ideas, and technical data. It will be up to you, the reader (or *user*) to decide whether or not I have met your design input criteria and your implied needs.

Developing this Manual was made easier thanks to the efforts of many friends and colleagues. First and foremost, thanks to Paul Webb, cofounder of XIS Consulting, Inc., who has shared in the belief of unleashing the value of ISO 9000 as a powerful management tool. His contributions to the philosophy behind the ideas in the Manual can be found throughout. He also spent considerable time in reviewing the material at various stages of its development.

Two versions of this Manual were reviewed by a number of "beta testers" who dedicated considerable time and energies to making "unauthorized changes" to controlled copies of this Manual as it was nearing completion (and without a concession)! The beta testers are listed in the Acknowledgments.

Help along the way has come from others who have been very supportive while the Manual was coming together. Sue Zegar and Lori Deibel have proved exceptional information experts whose assistance was much appreciated.

I was lucky to be able to call upon the talents of so many people.

Finally, thanks to my family for their constant support and encouragement, and to Courtenay Graham for her patience as I wrestled with completing this Manual!

James S. Davies

Acknowledgments

Mark Curran, Avalon
Imelda O'Connell, XIS Consulting, Inc.
Kinsley Binard, Geomatrix Consultants
Noel Ellis, XIS Consulting, Inc.
Samantha Munn, ITS Intertek Services
Jim Santos, Fidus Medical Technology
Eric Hunter, Network General Corporation
Ed Lambing, Hughes Aircraft Company
Reg Blake, BSI Quality Assurance

Charles "Pete" Bennett, Tandem Computers
Stan Salot, Hitachi
Courtenay Yates, Federal Reserve Bank
Andrea Lyle-Wilson, Hughes Aircraft Company
Joe Marchese, FirstWave
Bruce Blixt, MountainGate Data Systems
John Mraz, Quality Systems Associates
Robert Wright, Apple Computers
Rupert Kaufmann, Ernst & Young LLP

How to Use the Manual

Every reader will use this Manual in a subtly different way. What follows is a description of how it was designed to be used by quality and business professionals alike. It will provide you with ideas to help you maximize the benefit from the factsheets.

Structure of the Manual

With the exception of this introductory section, there are eight sections, each containing a number of different factsheets (Figure I-1).

These sections fall broadly into two main themes. The first part of the Manual provides a methodology for the implementation of a formal management system based around the ISO 9001 framework. The second part provides a suite of ISO 9001 Technical Factsheets, one or more for each clause of the standard. Together, these parts form an integrated approach to quality management and process management.

Business Management System Implementation

Provides material covering the design and implementation of an ISO 9001 Business Management System

ISO 9001 Technical Factsheets

Provides advice and guidance about interpreting, applying, and meeting the requirements of ISO 9001 (1994)

Figure I-1: Structure of This Manual

Navigating the Manual ❶

There are many ways to navigate quickly around the Manual. At the top of each factsheet is an individual reference number for that factsheet (Figure I-2). The letter refers to the section of the Manual. For example "T" refers to the Toolkit section, and "B" refers to the Background section. The number following the letter refers to the sequence of factsheets in a section. For example, "T-4" refers to the fourth factsheet in the Toolkit section.

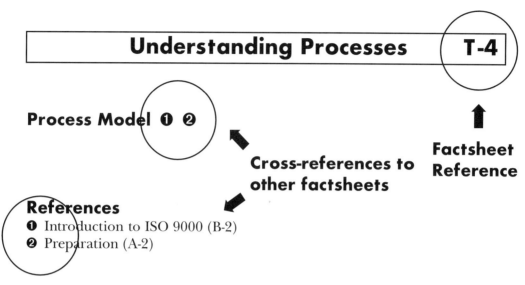

Figure I-2: Factsheet Cross-referencing

Where reference is made to a concept or tool elsewhere in the Manual, the factsheet provides a number by the side of the paragraph heading. This number means that at the end of the factsheet (under the References heading), there are other factsheets listed that you can refer to for further information or guidance.

The Quick Reference Guide provides a useful way of navigating the Manual, outlining which factsheets a section contains and the purpose of each factsheet. Further, an abbreviated reference guide is included with each section.

Tutorial

To help reinforce understanding of the material in this manual, a series of exercises are provided, one at the end of each section. These exercises are designed to be finished as the reader completes a section. Since each ISO 9000 project is different and each requirement of ISO 9000 is subject to similarly different interpretation, answers are not provided as such. The tutorial could equally be used as the basis of project team workshops. Using the factsheets in the book as background information, team members can discuss the exercises as a group.

Technical Factsheets

To understand the requirements of ISO 9001, there is a suite of Technical Factsheets that all follow a consistent format (Table I-1) and describe the clauses in some detail.

Minimum Requirements

The management system approach outlined in this Manual does not limit itself by the constraints of ISO 9000. Moreover, it does not consider that the minimum requirements of ISO 9000 alone provide a comprehensive management system infrastructure with which a company can improve and grow.

Section	Contents
Overview	Working overview of the element, including perspectives for understanding, interpreting, and applying that element
Documentation required	Some ideas about what documentation may be necessary to meet the requirements of the element
Implementation approach	Brief overview of how the element may be approached
Changes from ISO 9001 (1987)	List of the changes introduced in the 1994 version of the standard
References	List of associated factsheets

Table I-1: Sections within the Technical Factsheets

Instead, this Manual provides a blueprint for a Business Management System that calls upon ISO 9000 but supplements it with the necessary ingredients to ensure its effectiveness and long-lasting value. Therefore, those companies wishing to simply meet the minimum requirements of ISO 9000 will have to pay attention to the standard itself to clarify these requirements. When in doubt, always refer to the ISO 9000 standards themselves. Understanding the requirements of each ISO 9001 clause is often straightforward; learning to interpret and apply them for your organization is the challenge.

Service or Product? ❷

Despite the origins of ISO 9000 traceable to the manufacturing industries, and the higher adoption of ISO 9000 in the manufacturing sector rather than in the service industries, this Manual was wherever possible written with both industries in mind. When all is said and done, a service is a product that has to be designed, developed, produced, and delivered to a customer, just like a more traditional product, such as an electronic appliance. Although the terminology in ISO 9001 is more directed toward manufacturing, if you read beyond the text, it can be applied to services without difficulty. Additional guidance on interpreting ISO 9001 is available from ISO 9004-2, *Guide to Quality Management and Quality System Elements for Services.*

ISO 9001 or ISO 9002? ❸

To avoid the overuse of both standards within the Manual, a decision was made to simply reference ISO 9001, thereby covering all twenty elements (rather than just nineteen with ISO 9002). Companies adopting ISO 9002 should simply ignore any reference to the element Design Control (4.4), which is applicable only to ISO 9001.

References

❶ Quick Reference Guide
❷ Bibliography
❸ ISO 9000 Series Overview (B-7)

ISO 9000
Management Systems
Manual

ISO 9000
Management Systems

Background

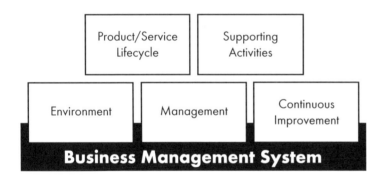

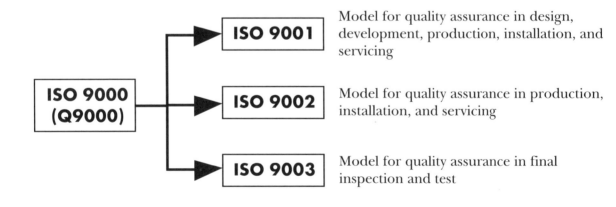

Foundation for the Future ❶

Companies are finding they need to be adaptive in order to be successful in remaining responsive and agile in the face of change. This pressure to change reflects the uncertainty in the business world—needs of stakeholders are changing, competition is greater in the global marketplace, and there is constant pressure to do more with less. In certain industries, companies find themselves having to conform with changing regulations and legislation.

It is becoming increasingly clear that quality management, and the operational systems that support it, go beyond simply assuring consistent product or service quality. Quality management can provide a foundation for the organization, helping to support this change. Such objectives are usually the *drivers* behind quality management (Figure B-1). Management systems need not simply form the basis for independent registration or compliance to established standards and regulations. The management system, if designed and implemented effectively, serves to provide a framework for greater management control and provides a powerful platform to support other management initiatives.

Figure B-1: Driving Forces Behind Quality Management

ISO 9001: Framework for a Management System ❷

The framework for the management system discussed in this Manual is based on ISO 9001 (1994), *Quality Systems–Model for Quality Assurance in Design/Development, Production, Installation, and Servicing*. ISO 9001 has been widely adopted across the world as the benchmark for effective management. Consisting of twenty elements, each with very specific requirements, ISO 9001 can be summarized in terms of the impact it has on an organization (Figure B-2).

Agree what you do	Analyze and map current practices
Say what you do	Define those practices in a formal management system
Do what you say	Ensure all staff follow the processes described in this system
Improve what you do	Drive continuous improvement

Figure B-2: What ISO 9001 Requires of an Organization

Before processes can be defined as part of a formal management system, they must be fully understood and mapped. Often these processes are not consistently performed, with variation between different groups or projects. The processes are defined and become a part of the management system in the form of process documents such as procedures and work instructions. These documents are an organizational statement of how processes are managed for consistency and repeatability. Next, an organization has to ensure that staff are following these processes, and this can be verified through internal audits of the management system and the use of metrics and other measurements. Finally, ISO 9001 expects evidence of continuous improvement of processes and products.

Limited Scope of ISO 9001 ❸

Considering Figure B-3 (adapted from ISO 9000-1), it is clear that only a certain degree of an organization's quality system is directly concerned with external quality assurance. ISO 9001 is primarily concerned with providing customers with confidence that their stated quality requirements will be met. For this reason, many organizations maintain a minimum quality system to meet customer requirements and industry regulations, thereby failing to capitalize on its potential in other areas. This is one way in which an organization fails to readily benefit internally from an ISO 9000 initiative.

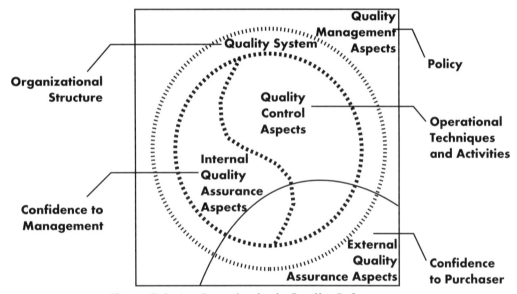

Figure B-3: An Organization's Quality Infrastructure

Business Management System ❹

This Manual does not attempt to address the theory behind quality, quality assurance, and quality management. Rather it outlines a philosophy about the way in which an effective management system can be structured and implemented to optimize the strengths of ISO 9001. The aim of the methodology outlined in this Manual is to show an organization what such a management system can achieve for an organization. The objective (or vision) is to achieve the foundation for a **Business Management System (BMS)** capable of supporting an organization through growth, change, and improvement.

Different Approaches ❺ ❻

There are many different approaches to implementing a management system based around a framework such as ISO 9001. Although every organization implements ISO 9001 in a subtly different way (Figure B-4) for good reasons, there are generally three accepted approaches.

First, some companies adopt the organization approach in which individual departments, groups, or sites are responsible for designing and implementing a management system based on functional groups rather than processes. This approach tends to constrain the quality system by imposing functional barriers, even though the breakdown of these cross-functional barriers is often one of the objectives of instilling quality management in an organization.

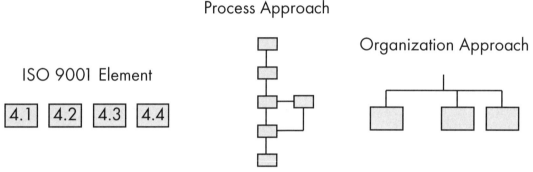

Figure B-4: Different Approaches to ISO 9001 Implementation

Another approach is to drive the initiative by compliance models such as ISO 9001, such that the quality system itself does not map directly to the way in which a company operates, but rather it maps to the specific structure and requirements of the model. Although this approach makes the process of independent assessment of the management system easier for an external organization like a registrar, it tends to produce a management system that adds limited value to a company.

Both of the approaches described above can be appropriate based on the availability of resources. However, the end result is a largely prescriptive management system that limits the added value of a formal management system. The approach advocated in this Manual is the third option—that of designing and implementing a process-driven quality system that largely ignores (or at least manages) cross-functional boundaries, and does not constrain itself by models such as ISO 9000. This type of approach helps to ensure that the resultant management system both reflects actual practice and adds value to day-to-day activities within an organization.

Customizing the Approach

Individual circumstances will always require an approach modified to meet the very individual needs of an organization and its culture. This Manual outlines a stable, effective approach to implementing a management system that is applicable to all sizes of organizations and all industries. Depending on factors such as senior management commitment and support for the project and the availability of internal resources, this approach should be customized wherever necessary to accommodate these factors.

From Here ... ❼ ❽

The remainder of the Background section includes a more detailed explanation of how ISO 9001 can be used to design a management system. It also begins to explain the standard itself. At the end of each factsheet, follow the references throughout the Manual to begin to build up a picture of the project. When you are ready to move forward, the next stage will be to start the methodology. The first phase, Preparation, addresses the need for effective communication and active management support. An Executive Summary factsheet is included as the first step.

References

❶ Preface (I-1)

❷ What Is ISO 9000? (B-5)

❸ Bibliography

❹ Business Management Systems (B-3)

❺ Organizational Environment (T-9)

❻ Overview of Project Approach (A-1)

❼ Using This Manual (I-3)

❽ Executive Summary (B-2)

What Is ISO 9000?

The International Organization for Standardization (ISO) adopted a British Standard BS 5750 as ISO 9000, signifying its acceptance as an international standard. The most comprehensive conformance standard in the series, ISO 9001 (Figure B-5), was revised in 1994. ISO 9001 requires an organization to design, implement, and maintain a Business Management System (BMS). It outlines a set of minimum requirements that must be met in order to claim compliance or attain registration. These requirements cover all aspects of a product or service lifecycle, from design (where appropriate) through manufacturing to post-sales support and installation.

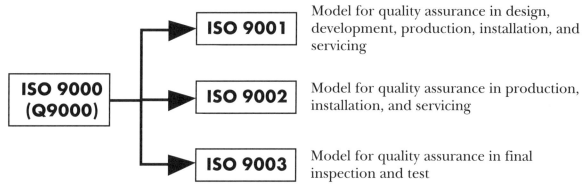

ISO 9001 — Model for quality assurance in design, development, production, installation, and servicing

ISO 9002 — Model for quality assurance in production, installation, and servicing

ISO 9003 — Model for quality assurance in final inspection and test

Figure B-5: ISO 9001 Is One of Three Conformance Standards in the ISO 9000 Series

Benefits of ISO 9000

To date, over ninety countries have adopted the standard and an estimated 100,000 certificates worldwide have been awarded to companies that have been independently assessed and registered against its requirements. In the 1990s, ISO 9000 is rapidly becoming the minimum requirement for doing business in both the US domestic market and international markets. As such, implementing ISO 9000 provides a company a powerful marketing edge over competitors. It also provides leverage in the marketplace, by helping market products or services in both the US and international markets. However, marketing is not the only benefit of ISO 9000 (Figure B-6).

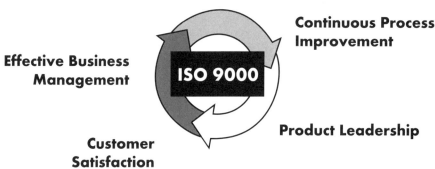

Operational Excellence

Continuous Process Improvement

Effective Business Management

ISO 9000

Product Leadership

Customer Satisfaction

Figure B-6: Internal Benefits of ISO 9000

These benefits affect the entire organization and involve all aspects of business management. By providing the framework for a management system, ISO 9000 also provides a management infrastructure to promote effective management. By instilling continuous improvement at the heart of the management system, it also provides the tools with which to measure and improve processes, toward the goal of operational excellence. The benefits of this process management can be felt during all stages of a product or service lifecycle, from design through delivery to the customer. A formal management system enables consistency in approach and effectiveness, helping to improve and innovate products.

All of these benefits represent improvement in one very important area: customer satisfaction.

ISO 9000 Business Management System

A formal ISO 9000 management system addresses the entire organization (Figure B-7). An organization typically designs, builds, and delivers a product or service. The process whereby this occurs is the **Product/Service Lifecycle.** The lifecycle depends on a number of other processes, such as purchasing, that enable designing and building the product. These processes are referred to as the **Supporting Activities.**

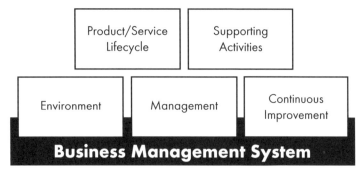

Figure B-7: Five Main Elements of ISO 9001

The infrastructure within ISO 9001 is comprised of Environment, Management, and Continuous Improvement activities. **Environment** refers to the operating environment, and in particular how information and knowledge are communicated, controlled, and made accessible to the organization. **Management,** on the other hand, refers to the management of the BMS rather than the information it oversees. Management defines the structure of the organization and its management, defines the responsibilities and authorities of staff, and also sets policy and objectives for the BMS. Finally, **Continuous Improvement** provides a closed-loop system whereby organizational performance against the BMS can be measured and improved.

Project Approach

The recommended approach involves designing and implementing a process-driven management system that adds maximum value to day-to-day activities within an organization.

There are six phases associated with the methodology (Figure B-8), from raising quality management awareness within the company and selecting a project team, through undergoing a registrar assessment to validate the effectiveness of the BMS against internal objectives and best-practice models such as ISO 9001.

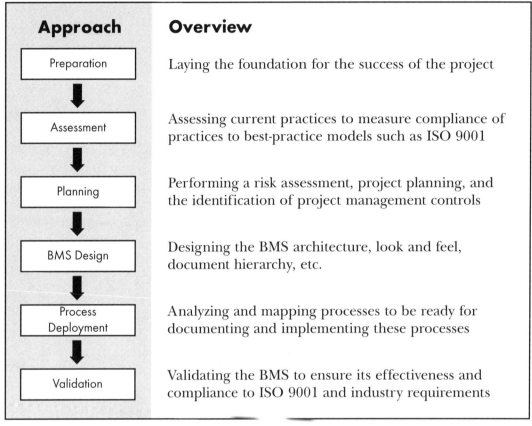

Approach	**Overview**
Preparation	Laying the foundation for the success of the project
Assessment	Assessing current practices to measure compliance of practices to best-practice models such as ISO 9001
Planning	Performing a risk assessment, project planning, and the identification of project management controls
BMS Design	Designing the BMS architecture, look and feel, document hierarchy, etc.
Process Deployment	Analyzing and mapping processes to be ready for documenting and implementing these processes
Validation	Validating the BMS to ensure its effectiveness and compliance to ISO 9001 and industry requirements

Figure B-8: Overview of the Project Approach

Introduction ❶ ❷ ❸

Although the need for an organization's quality policy to specifically address business objectives was introduced in ISO 9001 (1994), often quality management and business management systems don't readily converge. An analogy from ISO 10013 (*Guidelines for Developing Quality Manuals*) concerning the different types of quality manuals (and their roles) can be applied to a BMS. The standard discusses the difference between a *quality assurance manual* (one that can be shown to customers and doesn't contain any proprietary business information) and a *quality management manual* (containing proprietary information, such as goals and objectives, and not for use outside of the company).

Apply the same principles to a quality system and it suggests that a typical ISO 9001 quality system mainly addresses only quality assurance issues, and a business management system addresses quality management and business management as well. Converging the two approaches therefore provides an integrated **Business Management System** (BMS) that satisfies any compliance issues, but has at its heart the role of managing the business environment.

Blueprint for a BMS ❸ ❹

ISO 9001 is a very unfriendly standard! Understanding its structure is just as difficult as interpreting its requirements. It helps to think of it as having five main elements (Figure B-9). What an organization does typically is design, build, and deliver a product or service. The process whereby this occurs is the **Product/Service Lifecycle.** The lifecycle depends on a number of other processes, such as purchasing, that enable designing and building the product. These processes are referred to as the **Supporting Activities.**

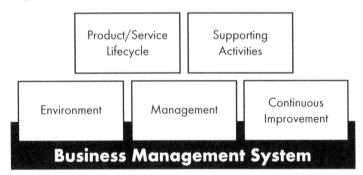

Figure B-9: Five Main Elements of ISO 9001

Companies often have some type of management control or even procedures describing either the lifecycle or the supporting activities. However, there is no infrastructure behind these controls, which makes them difficult to implement, measure, and improve.

The infrastructure within ISO 9001 is comprised of Environment, Management, and Continuous Improvement activities. **Environment** refers to the operating environment, and in particular how information and knowledge are communicated, controlled, and made accessible to the organization. **Management,** on the other hand, refers to the management of the BMS rather than the information it oversees. Management defines the structure of the organization and its management, defines the responsibilities and authorities of staff, and also sets policy and objectives for the BMS. Finally, **Continuous Improvement** provides a closed-loop system whereby organizational performance against the BMS can be measured and improved.

An effective business management system harnesses all available **enablers.** Rather than just becoming a stand-alone set of instructions, the BMS and its process management strengths can be found at the core of the organization. The BMS ensures effective deployment of resources such as staff, equipment, and materials. Striving for performance and automation, the BMS makes best use of technology, whether it be automated document management or intranets for record access. Last, but not least, the BMS harnesses the knowledge of staff across the company.

Figure B-10: Examples of Internal Enablers

By focusing on training and employee development, the BMS also provides an environment for gaining and sharing knowledge (the most valuable asset an organization can have).

Other Initiatives

Structuring the BMS around the way a company does business allows an organization to use the BMS to support a multitude of different improvement strategies and initiatives (Figure B-11). Implementation of these initiatives tends to be much more successful when supported by a business infrastructure such as the one proposed by ISO 9000. Many managers recognize the need to define practices and processes before sustained continuous improvement can really occur. The design and introduction of a BMS enables an organization to examine its processes and define them.

**Figure B-11: Examples of Initiatives Supported
by the BMS**

Such initiatives are typically conducted after the BMS has reached a suitable level of stability and maturity. Once a company enters a phase of management system maturity following ISO 9000 registration, these initiatives make ideal quality objectives for the BMS.

Take activity-based costing as an example. Few companies can really measure the quantifiable benefits of quality management system implementation, since quality costs are not meaningfully measured. Proving a quality system has brought many internal benefits can therefore be difficult. Using newfound understanding of critical processes and process analysis techniques, a company can adopt activity-based costing concepts and tools to understand how to improve and streamline processes to optimize efficiency and reduce cost.

Benefits of a BMS

There are widespread advantages for an organization that implements a BMS and these advantages can easily be linked to the driving forces described earlier in the Manual. These advantages and benefits go far beyond the marketing advantage associated with, for example, ISO 9000 registration (Figure B-12). In every facet of the organization, visible benefits will be noticed.

Figure B-12: Benefits of a BMS

Taking customer satisfaction as an example, having a better understanding of what the customer wants, and being able to consistently deliver products and services that meet or exceed their needs, lead to greater customer satisfaction. This impacts on an organization's ability to retain customers and also to win new ones, either by exploiting competitive advantage or diversifying into new markets.

Understanding and communicating these benefits, and moving minds away from just compliance and registration, will help to reinforce management support for the implementation of the BMS. It is also possible to implement performance measurements against these benefits to quantitatively demonstrate internal benefits obtained during implementation later in the project.

References

❶ Introduction (B-1)
❷ Bibliography
❸ ISO 9001 Roadmap (B-6)
❹ BMS Blueprint (B-4)

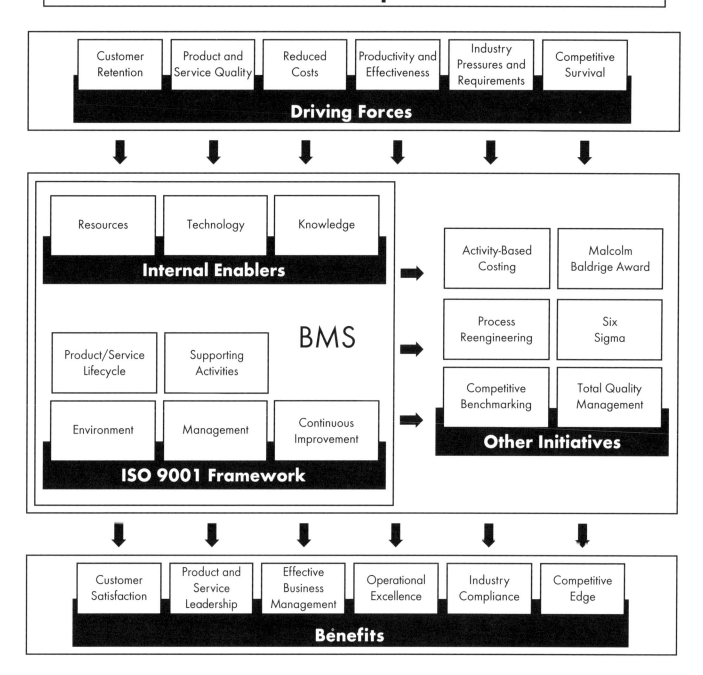

Driving Forces

- Customer Retention
- Product and Service Quality
- Reduced Costs
- Productivity and Effectiveness
- Industry Pressures and Requirements
- Competitive Survival

Internal Enablers

- Resources
- Technology
- Knowledge

ISO 9001 Framework

- Product/Service Lifecycle
- Supporting Activities
- Environment
- Management
- Continuous Improvement

BMS

Other Initiatives

- Activity-Based Costing
- Malcolm Baldrige Award
- Process Reengineering
- Six Sigma
- Competitive Benchmarking
- Total Quality Management

Benefits

- Customer Satisfaction
- Product and Service Leadership
- Effective Business Management
- Operational Excellence
- Industry Compliance
- Competitive Edge

Introduction ❶ ❷

In 1979, the British Standards Institution (BSI) published a National Standard, BS 5750, providing a framework for quality assurance. The origins of the standard, however, can be traced back to the US Department of Defense and the Mil-Q-9858A quality management program.

Although it was not written with third-party assessments in mind, the first company to seek registration to BS 5750 was a prefabricated concrete company. In 1987, BS 5750 was adopted and revised by the International Organization for Standardization (ISO) as ISO 9000, signifying its acceptance as an international standard. It has since undergone revision as part of a development path, and the revised standard was published in mid-1994 as BS/EN/ISO 9000. In the US, the national equivalent is ANSI/ASQC Q9000.

Since its original publication, the ISO 9000 series of standards has been widely adopted as an internationally accepted framework for quality assurance. To date, over ninety countries have adopted the Standard (Figure B-13), and an estimated 100,000 certificates worldwide have been awarded to companies who have been independently assessed and registered against its requirements. In the 1990s, ISO 9000 is rapidly becoming the minimum requirement for doing business in both the US domestic market and international markets.

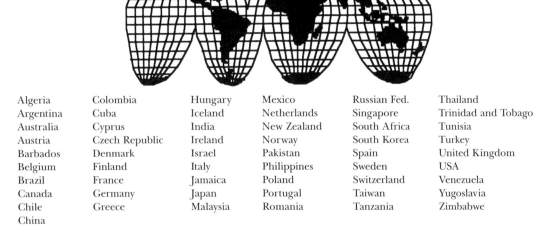

Algeria	Colombia	Hungary	Mexico	Russian Fed.	Thailand
Argentina	Cuba	Iceland	Netherlands	Singapore	Trinidad and Tobago
Australia	Cyprus	India	New Zealand	South Africa	Tunisia
Austria	Czech Republic	Ireland	Norway	South Korea	Turkey
Barbados	Denmark	Israel	Pakistan	Spain	United Kingdom
Belgium	Finland	Italy	Philippines	Sweden	USA
Brazil	France	Jamaica	Poland	Switzerland	Venezuela
Canada	Germany	Japan	Portugal	Taiwan	Yugoslavia
Chile	Greece	Malaysia	Romania	Tanzania	Zimbabwe
China					

Figure B-13: Increasing Worldwide Adoption of ISO 9000

Requirements of ISO 9000 ❸

ISO 9000 requires an organization to design, implement, and maintain a formal management system. It outlines a set of minimum requirements that must be met in order to claim compliance or attain registration. These requirements cover all aspects of a product or service lifecycle, from design (where appropriate) through manufacturing to post-sales support and installation.

There is also a number of quality system requirements to be addressed, such as document control and the need for internal quality audits. These elements of ISO 9001 or ISO 9002 (the difference is the provision of design) provide a framework for a formalized and effective management system.

In the ISO 9000 Standards, there is a number of terms that are commonly misunderstood when applying the content of the standards to a business (Table B-1).

Term	Explanation
Shall	Mandatory requirement that must be met
Should	Preferable or advised
Supplier	Organization seeking compliance
Customer	Customer of this organization
Subcontractor	Supplier to that organization of products and services
Where Appropriate	Discretionary

Table B-1: ISO 9001 Terminology

Benefits of ISO 9000

It is not just the marketing advantages and trade requirements associated with ISO 9000 quality system registration that motivate so many companies to pursue ISO 9000 and quality management. By using the framework and concepts of quality management as a management tool, benefits can be achieved across the entire organization, including:

✓ Increased customer satisfaction through heightened customer awareness and appreciation of quality across the organization
✓ Improved vendor performance through controlled supplier management
✓ Faster time to market through increased operational effectiveness
✓ Marketing edge and competitive advantage
✓ Increased consistency of processes across different functions
✓ Management system infrastructure for greater control
✓ Reduced cost of sale by eliminating non-value-added processes
✓ Sustainable continuous process improvement
✓ Reduced dependency on customer and supplier audits
✓ Foundation for other quality initiatives such as Total Quality Management (TQM)

The ISO 9000 Environment ❹

In order to demonstrate compliance with the ISO 9000 series, companies undergo an independent assessment by an organization known as a **registrar** (or certification body). A registrar is shown to be competent to operate within certain industries by being monitored through **accreditation.** Typically an accreditation agency will observe a registrar's assessment in a particular industry to ensure that the auditors used have the necessary experience and qualifications to understand the industry and the technology employed (Figure B-14).

Registration (the name given to the process of being successfully independently assessed by a registrar) involves an independent review of the quality system documentation, and an on-site assessment of the organization itself by certified quality auditors.

Depending on the findings from the assessment, a company can either be recommended for registration (in which case it can use certain registration marks on company literature and publicize its registration) or required to undergo a full or partial reassessment. The degree of reassessment depends on the nature and severity of the findings identified by the registrar.

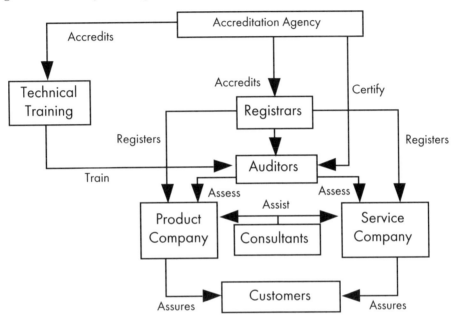

Figure B-14: The ISO 9000 Environment

US Market

The US accreditation agency is the Registrar Accreditation Board (RAB), which is affiliated with the American Society for Quality Control (ASQC), the National Institute for Standards and Technology (NIST), and American National Standards Institute (ANSI).

In the US, there has been widespread support for the standard, with the number of US registrations growing rapidly (circa 12,000 by end of 1996). Recently, the Food and Drug Administration (FDA) has revised the Good Manufacturing Practice (GMP) regulations to harmonize them with ISO 9001. With the EU directives and their requirements to market products in Europe, ISO 9000 has had a profound effect on many industries including the life sciences and healthcare industries. The US Department of Defense (DoD) has also announced support of the ISO 9000 series to help harmonize military and commercial quality systems conformity.

In the automotive industry, the Big Three manufacturers (Ford, General Motors, and Chrysler) have promoted QS 9000, a quality system conformity scheme based on the requirements of ISO 9000, and are requiring their first tier suppliers to conform to the standard.

These are just some examples of the support that ISO 9000 has received of late, in addition to government endorsement of the standard (for example, the Canadian government).

European Union (EU)

The predominant accreditation agencies are the United Kingdom Accreditation Services (UKAS), and the Dutch equivalent, Dutch Council for Accreditation (RvA). By far the most registrations to date are found in Europe and particularly the United Kingdom. Widespread adoption of ISO 9000 has meant that it has become the level playing field for doing business, irrespective of industry.

In the last few years, the European Union (EU) has introduced a series of EU-wide directives in such areas as medical devices, toys, and telecommunications. Directives recognize ISO 9000 for quality system conformity; gaining ISO 9000 registration and meeting certain product requirements leaves a product eligible to carry the CE mark to demonstrate conformity to a directive.

References

❶ Business Management Systems (B-3)

❷ ISO 9000 Series Overview (B-7)

❸ ISO 9001 Roadmap (B-6)

❹ Registrar Selection (T-3)

Model for the Twenty Elements of ISO 9001 ❶

Although ISO 9001 has many strengths and attributes, its structure is a considerable weakness. Comprised of twenty interrelated elements, many with subclauses, the standard is somewhat difficult to apply to activities an organization actually performs, whether it develops and manufactures product or designs and delivers a service. The key to understanding and applying ISO 9000 is to understand that these elements fall broadly into five main areas, each corresponding to a different aspect of an organization.

The **BMS Infrastructure** is the name given to the foundation that supports the management system. It consists of the **Environment,** comprised of systems for document control, record management, and staff training, together with **Management** activities (such as quality planning and policy making) and the different **Continuous Improvement** controls. These three areas provide the infrastructure to support the

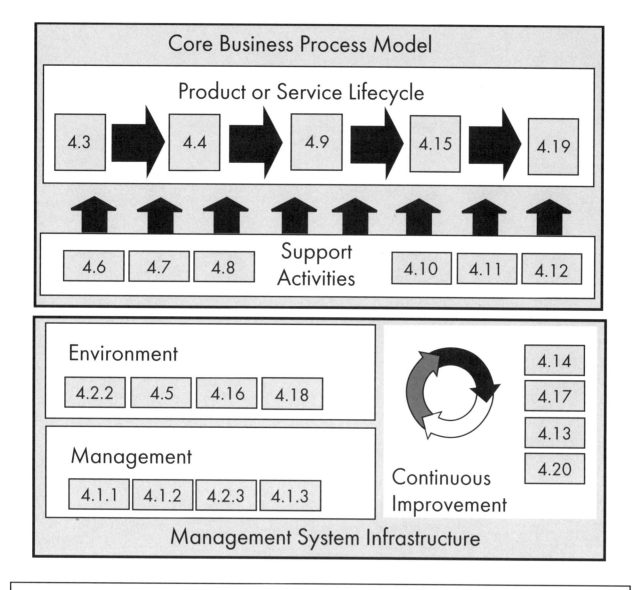

Core Business Process Model. This model represents the **Supporting Activities** (such as purchasing, inspection, and testing) which, in turn, support the **Product or Service Lifecycle.** It is this lifecycle that is at the heart of every business.

Key

Management responsibility (4.1), Quality system (4.2), Contract review (4.3), Design control (4.4), Document and data control (4.5), Purchasing (4.6), Control of customer-supplied product (4.7), Product identification and traceability (4.8), Process control (4.9), Inspection and testing (4.10), Control of inspection, measuring, and test equipment (4.11), Inspection and test status (4.12), Control of nonconforming product (4.13), Corrective and preventive action (4.14), Handling, storage, packaging, preservation, and delivery (4.15), Control of quality records (4.16), Internal quality audits (4.17), Training (4.18), Servicing (4.19), Statistical techniques (4.20).

References

❶ What Is ISO 9000? (B-5)

Introduction ❶

The ISO 9000 series of international standards provides a framework addressing the structure, function, and purpose of a product or service management system. This framework is generic and is, in addition to being applicable to all industries, equally applicable both to manufacturing product and delivering service.

The ISO 9000 family of standards falls into two categories: those dealing with quality management conformance and those offering guidance for the application of the standards. The guidance standards can be further divided between those that offer generic guidance on the application of ISO 9000, and those that interpret the requirements for a certain industry (industry-specific). Note that this factsheet does not address all members of the ISO 9000 series, since some standards are still in draft form.

Conformance Standards

There are three conformance standards in the ISO 9000 series (Figure B-15). Conformance standards are those that provide the basis for internal and external quality assurance where conformance to their requirements can be independently assessed.

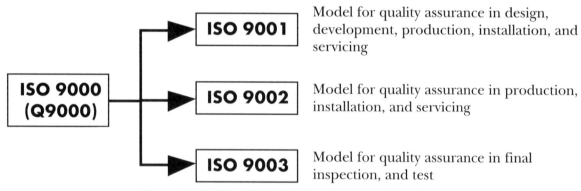

Figure B-15: The ISO 9000 Conformance Standards

ISO 9001 (1994)

Quality systems–Model for quality assurance, in design/development, production, installation and servicing.

This international standard is one of three detailing requirements defining the design, structure, and function of a BMS. It specifies quality *requirements* for use where a contract between two parties requires the demonstration of a supplier's capability to design and supply products or services. The requirements specified in ISO 9001 are aimed primarily at preventing nonconformity at all stages of a product or service lifecycle, from design through servicing. The standard addresses all stages of a product or service lifecycle.

ISO 9001 (1994) differs from ISO 9001 (1987) in a number of ways. In addition to providing clarity to the various elements of the standard, it also contains several new elements, including preventive action and quality planning. A greater emphasis on quality system documentation and the importance of quality records is also a feature.

ISO 9002 (1994)

Quality systems–Model for quality assurance in production, installation, and servicing.

This standard specifies quality system requirements for use where a supplier's capability to supply product conforming to an established design needs to be verified. Requirements specified in ISO 9002 are aimed at achieving customer satisfaction by preventing nonconformity at all stages from production through servicing but excluding design. The design element is the only difference between ISO 9001 and ISO 9002.

ISO 9003 (1994)

Quality Systems–Model for quality assurance in final inspection and test.

This international standard addresses the requirements for the detection and control of nonconformance during final inspection and testing. This standard applies to organizations whose conformance of products or services to specified requirements can be shown with adequate confidence, provided that the organization's capabilities for inspection and testing conducted on the product or service supplied can be satisfactorily demonstrated upon completion.

The revised 1994 edition contains more detailed requirements; it now includes many of the quality elements previously found only in ISO 9001 and ISO 9002.

Generic Guidance

General guidance on the application of the ISO 9000 series and on aspects of quality management is given in a number of different standards.

ISO 9000-1 (1994)

Quality management and quality assurance standards–Guidelines for selection and use.

This standard explains fundamental quality concepts. It defines key terms and provides guidance on selecting and applying ISO 9001, ISO 9002, and ISO 9003 for external quality assurance purposes (i.e., registration). It also provides guidance on using ISO 9004-1 for internal quality management purposes.

Essentially, this standard acts as a road map for the ISO 9000 family and has been expanded substantially in the recent revision. In particular, it contains guidance material and new concepts not in the ISO 9000 (1987) version. These additional concepts are needed to help ensure the understanding and effective application of the ISO 9000 series. Key concepts addressed in this standard include organizational objectives, process-driven organizations, and the role of quality system documentation.

ISO 9004-1 (1994)

Quality management and quality system elements–Guidelines.

This international standard provides guidance on quality management and quality system elements. The quality system elements are suitable for use in the development and implementation of a comprehensive and effective in-house quality system, with a view to ensuring customer satisfaction.

This standard is not intended for contractual, regulatory, or certification use. Consequently, it is not a guideline for the implementation of ISO 9001, ISO 9002, and ISO 9003. This is a revised edition of the ISO 9004 (1987) standard and reflects the need to better serve not only manufacturing but also process and service industries. More emphasis has also been placed on quality planning and preventive action.

Industry-specific Guidance

Two standards in the ISO 9000 series offer specific guidance to particular industries.

ISO 9000-3 (1991)

Quality management and quality assurance standards, Part 3–Guidelines for the application of ISO 9001 to the development, supply, and maintenance of software.

This member of the ISO 9000 series sets out guidelines to facilitate the application of ISO 9001 to organizations in the business of developing, supplying, and maintaining software (it is equally applicable to internal software design functions). It is intended to provide guidance when a contract between two parties requires the demonstration of a supplier's capability to develop, supply, and maintain software products.

ISO 9004-2 (1991)

Quality management and quality system elements, Part 2–Guidelines for services.

This part of the ISO 9000 series gives guidance for establishing and implementing a quality system within a service organization. Historically, ISO 9000 was intended for manufacturing industries but it is applicable to service organizations. ISO 9004-2 offers guidance on the application of the ISO 9000 conformance standards to those companies offering services to customers.

Other Useful Standards

ISO 10011 (1993)

Guidelines for auditing quality systems.

This standard is comprised of three parts and addresses key principles of quality auditing. Part 1 provides an overview of auditing and addresses audit objectives, the roles and responsibilities of the auditor team, and the audit process. Part 2 discusses the qualification criteria for auditors and discusses issues such as the training and experience required of auditors. Part 3 describes the audit process from planning and scheduling through the reporting of audit findings.

ISO 10013 (1993)

Guidelines for developing quality manuals.

This standard provides general advice on the content, structure, and format of quality manuals, one of the requirements of the conformance standards in the ISO 9000 series.

References

❶ Bibliography

Introduction (B-1)

What factors are driving the need for improvement in your organization? For each of the factors, explain how implementing an ISO 9000 management system will enable this improvement.

What are the industry or market requirements impacting your organization in the areas of management system certification or product certification? What marketing advantage would ISO 9000 registration provide?

What is management's understanding of ISO 9000 and the (positive) impact that it will have on an organization? Is management committed to provide the necessary resources that such a project will require?

Executive Summary (B-2)

What training will management need in order to ensure their understanding of the project before the project team is selected? What involvement will management have in the project, and what information should be communicated to them as the project proceeds?

Business Management Systems (B-3 and B-4)

What parts of your organization relate to the following parts of the Business Management System Blueprint?

(a) Product/Service Lifecycle

(b) Supporting Activities

(c) Environment

(d) Management

(e) Continuous Improvement

What other initiatives are either being considered by management or will be implemented during the course of the ISO 9000 project? How closely is ISO 9000 aligned with these initiatives?

In what ways can an organization expect to benefit from implementing an ISO 9000 management system? How should these benefits be communicated throughout the organization?

ISO 9000 Management Systems

Project Approach

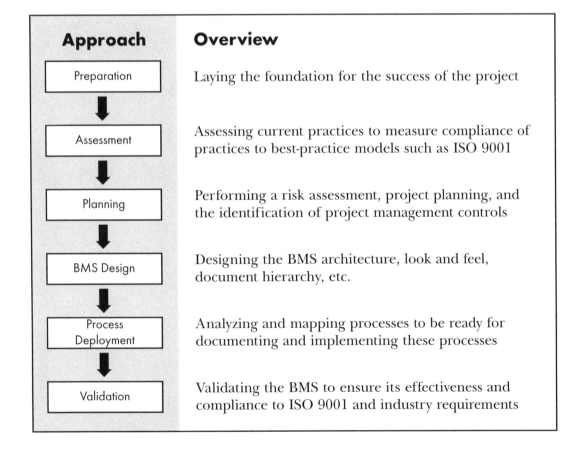

Approach	Overview
Preparation	Laying the foundation for the success of the project
Assessment	Assessing current practices to measure compliance of practices to best-practice models such as ISO 9001
Planning	Performing a risk assessment, project planning, and the identification of project management controls
BMS Design	Designing the BMS architecture, look and feel, document hierarchy, etc.
Process Deployment	Analyzing and mapping processes to be ready for documenting and implementing these processes
Validation	Validating the BMS to ensure its effectiveness and compliance to ISO 9001 and industry requirements

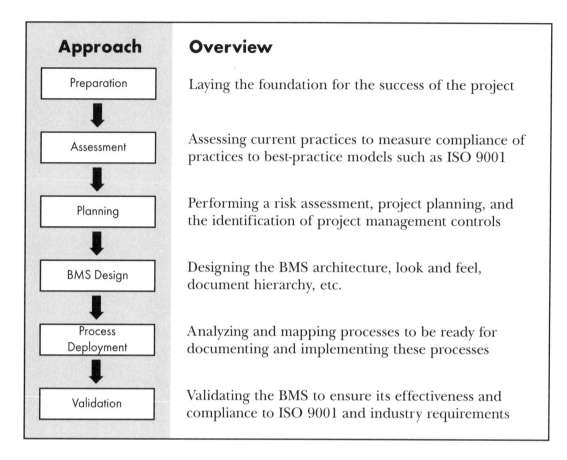

Approach	Overview
Preparation	Laying the foundation for the success of the project
Assessment	Assessing current practices to measure compliance of practices to best-practice models such as ISO 9001
Planning	Performing a risk assessment, project planning, and the identification of project management controls
BMS Design	Designing the BMS architecture, look and feel, document hierarchy, etc.
Process Deployment	Analyzing and mapping processes to be ready for documenting and implementing these processes
Validation	Validating the BMS to ensure its effectiveness and compliance to ISO 9001 and industry requirements

Phase	Inputs	Outputs
Preparation	Management decision to implement an ISO 9001 BMS	Established project team, communications plan, and ownership model
Assessment	Team training	Process data and compliance status
Planning	Assessment data	Risk assessment, project plan, and schedule
BMS Design	Assessment data	Designs for the BMS structure
Process Deployment	Established document hierarchy and templates, planning data, and background information	Deployed process documentation (such as procedures) and training
Validation	Partially or completely deployed management system	Formal management system compliant with ISO 9001

Preparation ❶

Before any work on the documentation can begin, it is necessary for the company to prepare for the project at hand. Implementing a management system can produce significant change within an organization and this change has to be carefully planned and controlled.

Initially it is necessary for management to establish a project team to oversee the development and implementation of the management system. The project team and management then work together to raise awareness throughout the organization of both quality management concepts and the forthcoming project, and help management define an ownership model and quality policy.

At this stage, some companies also elect to start a relationship with a third-party organization such as a registrar. This registrar will later assist the company in validating the system for effectiveness and compliance against industry models such as ISO 9000.

Assessment ❷

The first major task for the project team is to perform an assessment or review of current business processes. This review is comprised of a number of different steps, starting with the team collectively mapping the core business process model (also referred to as the product or service lifecycle) and then comparing this model with the specific requirements of best-practice models, including ISO 9001. This comparative analysis helps the team to understand how these external requirements apply to a company. Following this exercise, the team embarks on a more detailed survey of practices, looking specifically at the different systems and controls within each phase of the lifecycle (or each functional group).

The outcome of this survey is a list of processes identified as needing definition and documentation later in the project. This list is often prioritized according to operational feedback given by staff during the survey. By working at areas of known operational difficulty, the team is able to demonstrate visible benefits early in the project, further strengthening management support for the project.

Planning ❸

Taking the data from the assessment, the project team can work together to produce a project plan and schedule that will help manage the project through both the development of the BMS infrastructure and subsequent development of each individual process identified during the earlier assessment.

Combined with the disciplines associated with project management, the project plan allows the project to be carefully managed and tracked, thereby helping to ensure that management is kept abreast of project progress. This includes performing a risk assessment to determine where the project is at risk due to internal and external factors.

BMS Design ❹

Before individual processes can be researched and documented, the project team needs to design and develop the BMS infrastructure that will support both the individual business processes and the organization as a whole. The infrastructure requires that the structure and hierarchy of process documentation be defined, and infrastructure components (such as the continuous improvement and document control systems) be implemented. The infrastructure also includes a documented system for developing processes, starting from gathering background information on the process, researching each process with technical experts, and finally documenting the process for inclusion in the BMS.

Process Deployment ❺

With the BMS infrastructure in place, the project team can apply the process deployment approach to each individual process identified during the earlier assessment. The results of this approach are defined processes that are implemented into the management system. This deployment also involves providing training to staff in the areas of the system that are applicable to them. Such training helps to ensure that the management system will be followed by staff.

Validation ❻

Once the management system infrastructure and supporting business process documentation have been designed and implemented, it is time to begin to validate the effectiveness of the quality system and its compliance with industry requirements such as ISO 9000. Such validation includes the start of the internal audit program, using the corrective action system to drive the continuous improvement of the management system, and undergoing external assessments (for example, a registrar pre-assessment or an initial registration assessment).

References

❶ Preparation (A-2)

❷ Assessment (A-3)

❸ Planning (A-4)

❹ BMS Design (A-5)

❺ Process Deployment (A-6)

❻ Validation (A-7)

Approach

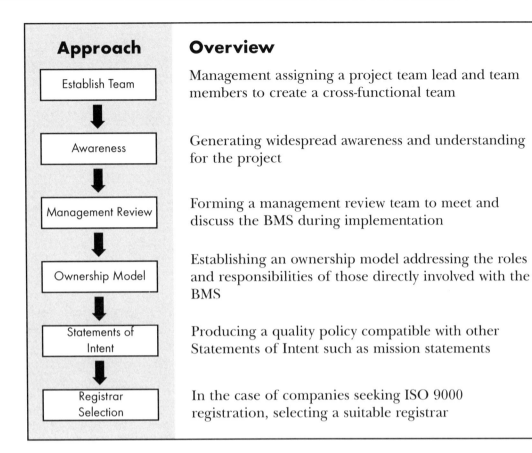

Establish Team

Awareness

Management Review

Ownership Model

Statements of Intent

Registrar Selection

Overview

Management assigning a project team lead and team members to create a cross-functional team

Generating widespread awareness and understanding for the project

Forming a management review team to meet and discuss the BMS during implementation

Establishing an ownership model addressing the roles and responsibilities of those directly involved with the BMS

Producing a quality policy compatible with other Statements of Intent such as mission statements

In the case of companies seeking ISO 9000 registration, selecting a suitable registrar

Phase	Inputs	Outputs
Establish Team	Management decision to implement an ISO 9001 BMS	Trained project team
Awareness	Review of different audiences and their communication needs	Communication model and supporting plan
Management Review	List of management team and a meeting agenda	Management review meeting minute and actions
Ownership Model	Management and team understanding of BMS roles, responsibilities, and authorities	Defined and documented ownership model addressing the BMS and management responsibility
Statements of Intent	Existing statements	Defined and agreed quality policy compatible with other statements
Registrar Selection	Responses to tender document and management presentations	Selection of a registrar that best meets a company's business needs

Introduction ❶

Preparation is the first phase in the project approach and arguably the most important, since it prepares a company for a project that will have a far-reaching impact across an organization.

Once a decision has been made to implement a management system, management will need to establish a project team that will steer the initiative. This team can then start to generate awareness for the project and begin to build the project foundation, which will help ensure the project's success. While awareness for the project is being communicated, management establishes a review team and agrees on an ownership model and quality policy under which to implement the management system.

Establishing the Project Team ❷

Management must select an experienced project team who will be responsible for designing and implementing the BMS. The project is usually managed by a project leader who is ultimately responsible for the project. This member of staff must have access to senior management to provide them with regular progress reports and early indication of problems that might impact on the project. It is important to understand that managing the project should not be confused with owning the BMS.

In addition to a thorough knowledge of the organization and its culture, the project team members supporting the project leader will require new training in a number of different areas relating to quality management and ISO 9001. Team members are usually representative of each key business area or organizational function within the company (and, in the case of multi-site companies, representative of different locations).

Generating Quality Awareness ❸

To ensure that the project is successful, it is critical to strengthen senior management buy-in and support from the start. Projects of this nature require extensive resources to be made available, not just to the project team, but to all staff within a company, whether it is the managers and engineers reviewing and approving new documents or other staff receiving quality awareness training. It is also executive management who will be establishing quality policy and other statements of intent. Once management has committed to the project, be it a result of market pressures for compliance to best-practice models, or a keen desire to improve practices, management needs awareness training in order to fully understand the project and its strategic importance to the company.

Quality awareness should not, however, be limited to senior management. A successful quality initiative requires the team to develop a communication model that addresses each different type of audience, internal and external. Based on this model, a communication plan can be produced and implemented to support the overall project.

Management Review ❹

During the early stages of the project, it is worth establishing with management the management review process that will be used to oversee both the implementation of the BMS and its maintenance after the Validation phase. This review process involves the collection of performance data pertaining to the management system. Such information is then reviewed by senior management to help determine its effectiveness.

By starting the management reviews early in the project, the project team can benefit from management involvement. In most cases, the more that management participates in the project, the greater its chances of success. One of the main reasons for ISO 9000 projects failing is a lack of visible and active management participation—in terms of leadership, commitment, support, and understanding. Management reviews go a long way in strengthening senior management involvement.

Ownership Model ❺ ❻

Working closely with the project team, management will need to agree on an ownership model that shows the various responsibilities and authorities associated with the implementation and subsequent maintenance of the BMS. There are many different schools of thought with regard to ownership (an example is given in Figure A-1).

It is the responsibility of management and the project team to communicate this model in order to ensure that the various groups and individuals identified in the model understand what is expected of them. The BMS ownership model is typically described in the quality manual or business manual. Similarly, provision needs to be made to support each level in the model to ensure that adequate resources are available to them. This is especially true during the Process Deployment phase later in the project.

Figure A-1: Example of an Ownership Model

For example, process owners often require the active involvement of technical experts to assist in developing their processes, and the quality manager requires sufficient responsibility and authority for effective decision making on matters relating to the management system. The old model of responsibility without the necessary authority to undertake the task will not work with such a model.

Statements of Intent ❼

ISO 9001 requires a company to define and communicate a quality policy that describes the organization's approach and commitment to quality and achieving customer satisfaction. Early in the project it is important for the project team to work with management to discuss and agree on a quality policy. Doing this early in the project helps set the overall direction of the project, provided the policy is well communicated across the company.

The vehicle for this exercise may take a variety of forms, ranging from the management review process to an executive briefing session. It is equally important to ensure that this quality policy is compatible with any existing statements of intent such as mission statements, charter, and vision and values.

Registrar Selection ❽

Most companies implement a management system based around an ISO 9000 framework for the purpose of gaining registration (or certification) to satisfy market requirements, both nationally and internationally. Since this process can take a number of months, it is important early in the implementation process to interview and select a registrar that meets not only the company's existing registration needs, but also future organizational needs and objectives.

This selection process, driven by the project team, involves collecting background information on registrars qualified to work in your industry, conducting interviews with representatives of the registrar, obtaining proposals for services, and finally (with the assistance of senior management), selecting the registrar that best matches a company's organization and culture.

References

❶ Overview of Project Approach (A-1)
❷ Establishing the Project Team (T-2)
❸ Generating Quality Awareness (T-1)
❹ Management Review (M-5)
❺ Organization (M-2)
❻ Process Deployment (A-6)
❼ Quality Policy (M-1)
❽ Registrar Selection (T-3)

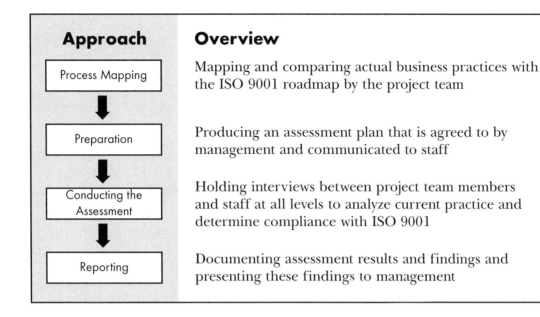

Phase	Inputs	Outputs
Process Mapping	Project team understanding of current practices in their functional area	Initial maps of the core business process model and BMS infrastructure, showing relationship with ISO 9001
Preparation	Initial maps and team responsibilities	Assessment schedules for project team interviews with Technical Experts
Conducting the Assessment	Assessment schedules and customized assessment form	Detailed assessment data supporting the initial maps
Report	Assessment data	Finalized assessment report

Introduction ❶ ❷

Assessment is the second phase in the project approach. Once project awareness has been raised across the company and a project team established, it is necessary to perform a diagnostic assessment before initial project planning can be started. The diagnostic assessment, performed by the project team, is sometimes also known as a *gap assessment* and provides the project with a baseline of understanding of current business practices. By studying existing processes, the team will be able to compare these processes with best-practice models (such as ISO 9000 and other industry requirements).

The objectives of this assessment are to provide the project with the following data, ready for project planning in the next phase of the project (Table A-1).

Objective	Explanation
Understand the Core Business Process Model	Gaining an understanding of how a product or service is taken from concept through delivery to the customer is critical for the project team. This flow of events is also referred to as the *lifecycle* and includes the *Supporting Activities.*
Identify Existing BMS Infrastructure	Study the organization to understand which elements of the BMS infrastructure already exist. This provides the project team with information ready for the design of the final BMS later in the project.
Operational Feedback	Gather concerns, operational issues, and improvement suggestions from staff during interviews and discussions. This feedback will help to identify early opportunities for improvement and allow the processes identified in the assessment to be prioritized based on staff feedback.
Existing Compliance	Determine the degree of compliance of current business practices against best-practice models such as ISO 9001.
Existing Documentation	Identifying what process and quality documents already exist helps the project team to estimate the resources required to document the current system. It also identifies valuable reference material for use when studying individual processes later in the project.
Create Awareness	Raise awareness of quality management concepts and the purpose of the project to staff across the organization.

Table A-1: Assessment Objectives

Process Mapping ❷ ❸ ❹

Using a workgroup session, the cross-functional project team can collectively identify the core business process model and the existing BMS infrastructure. The outcomes of this exercise are initial process maps, typically in the form of detailed flowcharts. These maps form the basis of the next part of this phase: comparing these maps with the actual requirements of ISO 9001 and any other industry requirements.

Where a company has to consider more than one model, the assessment (and for that matter, the entire Manual) can be tailored to accommodate these models, resulting in a management system that can meet all regulatory and industry requirements. Throughout the Manual, the models are referred to as **best-practice models.** For example:

✔ National or international guidance standards such as ISO 9000-3 for software development

✔ Industry-specific models such as QS 9000 for the automotive industry

✔ Industry regulations such as the Food and Drug Administration Good Manufacturing Practices (GMP) for the life sciences, food, and pharmaceutical industries

With the initial maps of the business model and infrastructure, the project team can perform a comparative analysis to begin to understand how existing practice differs from the requirements of the best-practice models. The purpose of this review is not to obtain a detailed understanding of where nonconformities may exist—that is the purpose of the interviews later in this assessment. Rather it is to understand how the guidance and/or requirements of these best-practice models can be mapped to the individual company's business practices. This helps project team members to start to interpret requirements in these models in the areas they have been assigned in the project.

Typically, this comparative analysis results in the production of matrices or charts that will later form an integral part of the quality manual or business manual.

To map out the core business process model and the BMS infrastructure, the project team must understand processes and their importance to an organization. There are many tools provided in this Manual to assist the team in selecting a system or individual process and analyzing it against certain characteristics.

Preparation ⑤ ⑥ ⑦

Using a workgroup, the project team can divide the functional groups, core business process model, and BMS infrastructure elements among the project team members. Depending on the size of each area, the team can also determine the number of person days required for the assessment. Unlike internal auditing (4.17), it is actually preferable that the team members assess and research their own departments or process areas. The success of the assessment is in part dependent on the team member being able to successfully map and flowchart individual processes, activities, and, in some instances, tasks that comprise these areas. This requires a thorough knowledge of the processes, which both the team member and **technical experts** possess. This exercise will also help identify which functional areas may later be excluded from the scope of the project. For example, human resources and finance are typically omitted from the scope of an initial assessment.

As soon as dates have been agreed upon between senior management and the project team, they are communicated across the company to help ensure the availability of managers and staff, and also to start generating project awareness. At this stage, more detailed planning is required before the assessment can begin.

Although some of the assessment will involve team members simply calling upon experience and researching information, interviews will also be necessary with staff throughout each area, and at all levels. Each project team member should schedule short interviews (1–2 hours) with staff knowledgeable in the areas they have been assigned—technical experts. These interviews form the basis of the schedules for individual team members during the assessment.

It is important to make the organization aware of *what* the project team will be doing and *why* during the assessment. Understanding and support for the assessment has to be seen at all levels within a company, so the earlier the awareness program starts, the better. The levels to address as part of this preparation phase are senior management, the project team (providing additional training where necessary), middle management, and remaining staff. The better the organization understands the assessment, the more valuable the data that it will provide.

As part of preparation, the project team can take the Assessment Form provided and customize it to meet the individual needs of the project. Thought should be put into the design to ensure that as much of the data as possible is quantifiable; that is to say that the data can be easily collected and analyzed after the assessment, and made ready for the Planning phase.

The Assessment Form assumes that each project team member has been assigned an area—be it a functional area (such as a group or department) or a process area (that may span several functional areas). It provides some ideas about what information can be obtained through the assessment interviews. The essential information to obtain from the interviews is:

✔ Summary of existing compliance with ISO 9001 and other models, identifying main areas where business practices do not meet the minimum requirements of the models

✔ Complexity of each process, in terms of the degree of existing documentation and the nature of the process

Conducting the Assessment ❼

A briefing meeting should be held a week before the assessment in which the details of the assessment will be confirmed and any scheduling difficulties discussed. Depending on approach, such a meeting could also be used to provide the project team with training in understanding processes, how to perform the assessment, and the use of the Assessment Form.

Working from the schedule prepared earlier, each project team member conducts interviews and records findings and interview notes on the Assessment Form.

At the end of each assessment day, summary meetings should be held between the project leader and team members to analyze the day's results. Some problems may have been encountered and these issues can be discussed as a team; sometimes a change in approach may need be considered to overcome issues and ensure the value of the data obtained from the assessment.

At the end of the assessment, all completed Assessment Forms and other data should be submitted to the project leader for collation and review.

Reporting

Once all results have been collated, the project team can begin to review and analyze the data. In addition to team members producing individual reports on each key area (based on the data from individual Assessment Forms), a summary report should be produced by the project leader. It is this summary report that is presented to upper management and management within each area.

Providing a brief report of the findings to staff across the entire organization should be considered in order to strengthen buy-in and understanding of the project. An internal memo from senior management and a presentation cascaded through staff meetings both act as good vehicles by which to communicate this information.

References

❶ Overview of Project Approach (A-1)
❷ ISO 9001 Roadmap (B-6)
❸ Understanding Processes (T-4)
❹ Process Mapping (T-5)
❺ Project Gantt Chart (T-8)
❻ Generating Quality Awareness (T-1)
❼ Assessment Form (T-6)

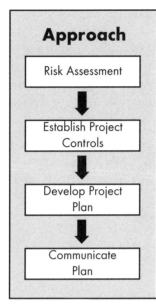

Approach

Overview

Analyzing of risks and identification of mitigation strategies to help manage and monitor risks associated with the project

Establishing project management controls for the project and the operation of the project team

Developing a detailed project plan for subsequent phases of the project

Communicating the project plan across the company

Phase	Inputs	Outputs
Risk Assessment	Finalized assessment report and data	Risk assessment and mitigation report
Establish Project Controls	Project team ground rules and team structure	Established project controls
Develop Project Plan	Finalized assessment report and data	Detailed project plan and schedule addressing the deployment of processes
Communicate Plan	Detailed project plan and schedule	Widespread awareness of the plan and schedule across company

Introduction ❶ ❷

Planning is the third phase in the project approach. Based on the assessment results, the project team and management must work together to produce a project plan corresponding to the remaining phases of the project approach: namely, the design and implementation of the BMS infrastructure, the deployment of each business process identified from the assessment, and validation activities to ensure that the management system is effective and compliant once implemented. Addressing any risks that the project team believe may impact on the project, this project plan defines the milestones, targets, and schedule for the remaining phases during which the BMS infrastructure and core business process model will be defined and documented.

This project methodology suggests project planning occurs after the assessment when, provided the assessment was effective, much data was collected and is available to the project team. The earlier phases of the project should not be exempt from the same type of planning.

Performing a Risk Assessment

Irrespective of the skills and experience of the project team, a project of this nature has many dependencies and risks associated with it. Due to the scale of this project, it is best practice to perform a risk assessment before planning the rest of the project. Once the project team has produced a comprehensive list of risks, each risk is analyzed using the following criteria and summarized in a report for management. This report should be reviewed on an ongoing basis as part of risk mitigation.

Each risk identified by the team should be described in terms of scope and context of the project. Depending on the nature of the risk, it should be assessed in terms of its potential impact to the project. Usually a score is assigned against each risk, for example, low (1), medium (5), or high (10) risk. The members of the project team then each take responsibility for a risk. It is this individual who will determine how best to monitor that risk, and what type of mitigation would reduce the risk.

An example of risk assessment against these criteria can be found in Table A-2 below.

Criteria	Risk
Description	Lack of management support (10)
Context	Perceived lack of proactive and visible support by management will not send the right messages to middle management and staff who will be actively involved later in the project during Process Deployment.
Responsibility	Management Sponsor, Project Leader
Monitoring	Weekly project meetings and management meetings
Mitigation	Additional training and awareness to increase understanding of the BMS

Table A-2: Example of Risk Assessment

Once this exercise has been completed for all the risks identified by the team, the project lead should summarize the risk assessment in the form of a report that is presented to senior management. Care should be taken to ensure that these risks are tracked throughout the project to avoid false starts with the project.

Establishing Project Controls ❸

Implementing a management system is a major undertaking for an organization, not least of all because it impacts most functions and processes within an organization. Many organizations fail to understand the magnitude of such a project, both in terms of the resources and commitment required to ensure its success, and the impact it will have upon the organization.

For this reason, it is important that a project of this nature be carefully managed, controlled, and monitored. Project management tools and techniques should be employed to help maximize the use of internal resources and minimize project costs. Many organizations use project management software to manage projects and initiatives of this type. The project is usually performed under the controls of project management, using the phases within this methodology as simple milestones. These controls include maintaining project plans as current, resource allocation and tracking, deliverables, and the need for regular project team reviews with senior management.

Developing the Project Plan ❷ ❹ ❺ ❻

The assessment performed earlier in the project provided much project data that will need to be collected and analyzed by the project team. It is now necessary to take the list of processes identified in the assessment and assign each process an owner. This process owner may or may not be either a project team member or technical expert who took part in the interviews during the assessment. In the case of more complex processes, ownership may even be given to a group. For example, a process may span several functional groups and may benefit from closer coordination than would be needed for a simple process that occurs within a single functional group.

Each process owner is required to follow the Process Deployment methodology, which involves analyzing the process using the assessment data, mapping it, and producing documentation to support it. The project plan needs to address the amount of effort required in following this methodology, as this forms the basis of the project plan. There are many factors that will affect the resources required in defining and deploying a process, including:

✔ Complexity of the process
✔ Amount and accuracy of any existing documentation
✔ Resolving any noncompliances identified in the assessment
✔ Amount of training required before deploying the process

Given these factors, the project team must create a planning matrix that defines the elapsed time required for each type of document in the BMS document hierarchy. An example of such a matrix can be seen in Table A-3, which addresses a procedure of moderate complexity. The figures used in the plan can be customized to suit both the complexity of the process and the amount of resources that the process owner can dedicate to the exercise.

Document Type	Research and Analysis	Process Mapping	Process Definition	Release and Implementation	Total
Procedure	5 days	5 days	10 days	10 days	30 days
Instruction	5 days	5 days	5 days	5 days	20 days
Form, checklist, or template	1 day	1 day	5 days	5 days	12 days

Table A-3: Example of Planning Matrix

By applying the different templates and guidelines given in this manual, the process owner can determine the level of resources and elapsed time needed to generate the appropriate process documents. An example can be seen in Table A-4, where the matrix has been applied to the process of internal quality audits.

Process	Document Name	Document Type
Planning Audits	Planning an Internal Audit Annual Audit Schedule	Procedure Form
Conducting Audits	Conducting an Internal Audit Audit Checklist Audit Trail Nonconformity Report	Procedure Checklist Form Form

Table A-4: Internal Quality Audits

When planning all the remaining phases of the project, there are many other factors that will influence the length of time and the internal resources that will be required for the project. These factors to consider include:

✔ Management buy-in and support
✔ Internal resources and budget allocated to the BMS
✔ Skills and knowledge of the project team
✔ Extent of external consulting assistance
✔ Market pressures for registration
✔ Factors such as multisite locations, commonality between locations, etc.

In addition to these factors, it is important to consider other internal aspects that may impact on the project. Examples include the end of the financial year and the annual inventory (where applicable). Consideration should also be given to the registrar selection process, which can take an elapsed time of several months from initial contact to final selection. Any preassessments or initial assessments planned with a registrar will need to be included as milestones for the initial project plan.

Communicating the Plan

The completed project plan will need to be communicated regularly to senior and middle management. In addition, a simplified plan with clear milestones should be communicated to all staff to keep awareness of the project high.

The project lead is responsible for maintaining project plans as current throughout the development cycle, with changes made according to new information received. For example, significant process changes may be required, either as a result of improvement opportunities or to meet the requirements of the best-practice models such as ISO 9001. When the project plan or schedule change, the project lead must communicate these changes.

References

❶ Overview of Project Approach (A-1)

❷ Assessment (A-3)

❸ Establishing the Project Team (T-2)

❹ Project Gantt Chart (T-8)

❺ Process Deployment (A-6)

❻ Registrar Selection (T-3)

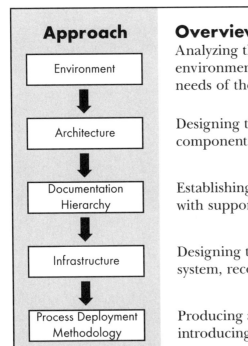

Approach	Overview
Environment	Analyzing the organizational and operational environment to ensure that the BMS will reflect the needs of the environment
Architecture	Designing the future BMS, showing how the various components of the BMS will integrate and interact
Documentation Hierarchy	Establishing the different levels of documentation, with supporting document templates
Infrastructure	Designing the BMS infrastructure: document control system, records management, and training processes
Process Deployment Methodology	Producing a set of integrated processes for introducing new documentation into the BMS

Phase	Inputs	Outputs
Environment	Assessment data	Understanding of the organizational and operating environment
Architecture	Assessment data	High-level BMS design
Document Hierarchy	Types of existing documentation identified during the assessment	Defined document hierarchy with clear purpose, scope, and format for each type of document
Infrastructure	Assessment data	Designs for document control, records management, training, continuous improvement, and management responsibility
Process Development Methodology	Assessment data	Documented methodology for defining and implementing a process

Introduction ❶

Designing the Business Management System (BMS) is the fourth phase of the project approach. It builds upon the foundation provided by the Preparation, Assessment, and Planning phases, and in particular the assessment of business practices. Once a company fully understands both what it has in place already and what is required by models such as ISO 9000, the next step is to design and implement some of the core elements to support the development of the management system as a whole.

Designing the management system is arguably critical to the project's long-term success. Careful consideration should be given to the infrastructure within the management system; a strong foundation ready for implementing individual processes will greatly assist the process owners in their responsibilities.

Studying the Organizational Environment ❷

Before work begins with the system, the project team can meet to discuss the organizational environment that will both support and be supported by the management system. These workgroup discussions should include organizational structure, technology, and culture.

By structuring an organization more around key processes, it follows that change will primarily be process-driven, and not organization-driven; results will encourage continuous improvement and the success of the project. When the project team discusses this issue, it should explore ways in which the company can become more process oriented, and ensure that the management system design is built around processes and not organizational structure.

Technology is another issue that the project team needs to consider before designing the BMS, since there are many advantages to harnessing available technology to support the initiative.

Last, but not least, the project team should review the company's culture to determine any cultural constraints on the BMS. Even the best management system in the world, unless it has the support of staff across the company, will never fulfill its potential. The project team should address such issues as the way in which the system is presented to staff, user-friendliness of documents, simple navigation around the management system, and the use of graphics and flowcharts to reinforce understanding.

Architecture ❸ ❹ ❺

Taking the results from the environmental survey and the assessment, the project team can be split into task teams charged with designing the overall structure and architecture of the BMS. The ISO 9001 Roadmap in this Manual demonstrates how a typical company operates, and serves as an example of a simple management system architecture, illustrating how it can be organized and presented as a collection of modules that interact to form an integrated business system.

Another example, shown in Figure A-2, represents a company that manufactures computer storage devices. The lifecyle for a new product begins with either a new business opportunity being identified, or a Statement of Work (SOW) being received from a customer.

Once the marketing organization has defined the product features in a marketing requirements document (MRD), the project moves into engineering, which is responsible for the design and development of the product. When the product has been fully tested and validated, it passes into the production organization ready for manufacturing. Each end product is then delivered directly to the customer, supported by value-added services such as installation and training. For the life of the product, the company provides post-sales support.

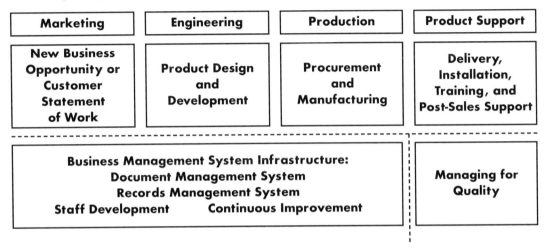

Figure A-2: Example of a BMS Architecture

In this example, the company supports the varied nature of the projects by implementing process libraries in the engineering department. The libraries allow the design engineers and project managers to work together to define an optimal (but realistic) approach that can be tailored to individual projects.

Although quality is embedded and distributed across all processes, a central group manages the BMS day-to-day activities, such as the collection of company performance metrics, document control, and the maintenance of the continuous improvement systems.

Consider any operation interfaces with parts of the organization that, for whatever reason, are excluded from the initial scope of the BMS. There are many different organizational areas that may be included only in part from the start of the project. For example, Human Resources may be included in the project scope for training (4.18), but excluded for other responsibilities such as performance appraisals, hiring new staff, and arbitration. Other functions typically outside the scope of the initial assessment include legal, finance, and facilities management.

Types of BMS Documents ❻

BMS documents are usually structured in a hierarchy according to the level of detail required by the reader. At the top of the pyramid are high-level strategic documents that describe the organization and provide an introduction to the management system. Most companies use a quality manual or business manual to fulfill this purpose and include company policies and statements of intent. All key components in the management system, such as the document control system, are described in guides that include an introductory overview (or roadmap) to that component. The guide is supported in turn by procedures that address individual processes and provide a more detailed description of the process flow, responsibilities, and tasks.

At this point, it is worth noting that very few companies use guides. Instead some companies use high-level procedures and, more often than not, just support a quality manual with a long list of procedures! Guides are simply an overview or description of a system, and help introduce structure to a management system.

While procedures contain specific requirements at a process level, instructions provide requirements relating to an individual task or activity conducted as a part of the overall the process. Both procedures and instructions are supported by forms, checklists, and templates that capture process and product data records. Finally, all these types of quality documentation are supported by standards and reference material. Standards may be internal, for example, providing guidance on company document formatting standards and house style, or a code of ethics. Reference material includes general documents outside of the company's control, such as national and international standards and customer and supplier documents.

Once an appropriate documentation structure has been agreed to and defined, templates can be produced for each type of document identified. These templates not only ensure a level of consistency between documents, but also save time when creating new documents.

Designing the BMS Infrastructure ❼

An effective BMS design consists of several key components, each of which serves a different purpose. Supporting the entire quality system is a core infrastructure that provides the platform on which the BMS can be developed, implemented, and maintained. Examples of systems within the infrastructure include:

✔ Document control system
✔ Records management system
✔ Staff training program
✔ Management activities such as quality planning and policy setting
✔ Continuous improvement processes and systems

Note that some companies work on less critical elements of the infrastructure while work begins on some of the key business processes.

Process Deployment Methodology ❽

Once the management system structure and a document hierarchy have been determined and adopted by the project team and management, it is necessary for the project team to define a method for researching, developing, producing, and releasing these documents. This methodology is then applied to all new quality documents that enter the management system, and helps to ensure consistency in approach between project team members and any other staff assigned ownership of processes.

References

❶ Overview of Project Approach (A-1)

❷ Organizational Environment (T-9)

❸ ISO 9001 Roadmap (B-6)

❹ Process Libraries (T-13)

❺ Managing Internal Interfaces (T-14)

❻ BMS Documentation (T-11)

❼ Designing the BMS Infrastructure (T-10)

❽ Process Deployment (A-6)

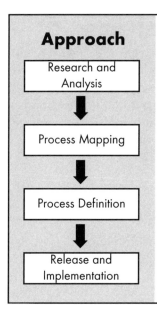

Approach

Overview

Research and Analysis
Detailed process data collected from interviews and work groups, and analyzed by the project team members

Process Mapping
Process model produced and validated for effectiveness and accuracy

Process Definition
BMS documentation produced to define the process model, and a rollout plan established

Release and Implementation
BMS documentation reviewed, approved, and released, and the process implemented using the rollout plan

Phase	Inputs	Outputs
Research and Analysis	Assessment data and existing documentation	Initial process maps
Process Mapping	Initial process maps	Detailed process maps discussed and validated with Technical Experts
Process Definition	Detailed process maps and existing documentation	Draft new documents based on process maps
Release and Implementation	Draft new documents based on process maps	Final new documents reviewed, approved, and implemented

Introduction ❶ ❷

Process deployment is the fifth phase in the project approach outlined in this Manual. Note that this process development methodology is applied to all processes within the core business process model, supporting processes, and the BMS infrastructure itself. In fact, once the BMS documentation structure has been established, the first process documents produced in the project should document this methodology and other aspects of the BMS infrastructure.

This process development methodology uses all available background information to date in order to produce an initial process map. This map is then used as the basis for interviews with technical experts who are involved in the process in day-to-day activities. Taking the interview data, the model is updated and reviewed again until it is ready for more definition.

Research and Analysis ❷ ❸ ❹

During the assessment phase, the project team collected considerable data relating to the many different systems and processes across the company. This data has been used already to plan what documentation needs to be written by the process owner assigned to work with the project team members to develop this documentation. The data also includes a list of technical experts who are knowledgeable about the process.

The process owner should first of all gather all background data relating to that process. Such information may come from a variety of sources, including:

✔ Assessment data obtained earlier in the project
✔ Documented results of previous internal improvement initiatives
✔ Existing documentation identified during the assessment

Based on this data, it should be possible to develop a high-level process map showing work flow. Such a map will describe the process and illustrate its relationship with other processes or systems. It is used later to focus the process owner and technical experts during interviews.

The process owner can also compare the map with best-practice models to identify any process changes that may be necessary in order to comply with these models.

Process Mapping ❸ ❹

Using the process form to capture information and the initial process map to keep the meeting focused, the process owner has two choices for validating the process model. One route involves individual interviews with technical experts and the second route involves a work group. If process owners are presented with the opportunity to assemble technical experts (and managers) for a work-group session, they should use the chance both to gain the necessary process data and to build consensus for any necessary changes to achieve compliance.

Once all the interviews have been conducted or the work group complete, the process owner will be able to update the initial process map into a more detailed map showing responsibilities, input, output, decision gates, etc. This map then goes through an iterative cycle of consensus building until all those involved with the process have agreed to the detailed process map. At this point, the process owner can begin to think about generating the necessary BMS documents to define the process.

Although quality management strives for consistency, quality management must equally allow for flexibility. One process approach across different groups may appear to streamline the process, but sometimes different groups have different needs, and for good reasons. The process documentation should allow for this variation, especially when the concept of process libraries has been adopted.

Process Definition ❺

As soon as the detailed process map is stable and agreed upon, the process owner should consider what implementation support will be necessary when the formal process is implemented. Collectively, the project team and managers should discuss implementation to help guarantee both the acceptance of the process by staff and also their understanding of the process. Based on these discussions, the project team should make provisions for (and plan) this implementation support.

Using the detailed map, the process owner (or designated author) can begin to prepare the necessary process documentation. This documentation may take a number of different forms, depending on the process and the degree of detail required for the process to be consistent. The project plan itself should contain an initial list of documents associated with each process. This documentation will typically include:

✔ Procedures
✔ Instructions
✔ Forms, checklists, and templates

To make sure that the draft documents are ready for review without the need for more than cosmetic changes, the process owner can release the draft documents into the document control system for review and approval. Achieving this level of confidence is possible if those affected by the document's content are able to review the last few versions of the draft document.

Note that the owner should ensure that other records and lists are updated. For example, if the process produces formal quality records, any central or local lists of records will need to be updated. Introducing process documentation may also produce ripple effects in other areas of the quality system, and this will need to be carefully managed.

Release and Implementation

Once complete, the draft documents enter the document control system ready for review and approval by staff members, representative of all groups, and individuals (including representative technical experts). Part of the assessment data includes a list of reviewers.

At the same time, any deployment support should be introduced. This may include, for example, training or awareness sessions for staff, the introduction of new tools associated with the process, and ensuring that all staff associated with the process have adequate access to the process documentation.

References

❶ Overview of Project Approach (A-1)
❷ BMS Design (A-5)
❸ Process Mapping (T-5)
❹ Process Form (T-7)
❺ BMS Documentation (T-11)

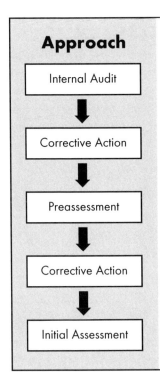

Approach	Overview
Internal Audit	Starting the internal quality audit program to ensure the BMS is effective and compliant with ISO 9001
Corrective Action	Performing corrective and preventive action to address the findings resulting from the internal quality audits
Preassessment	Undergoing a formal assessment to determine readiness for an initial assessment
Corrective Action	Performing corrective and preventive action addressing the findings resulting from the preassessment
Initial Assessment	Undergoing an external assessment by a registrar to determine whether the BMS is compliant to ISO 9001

Phase	Inputs	Outputs
Internal Audit	Trained internal auditors and audit schedule	Nonconformities, observations, and improvement suggestions
Corrective Action	Nonconformities raised during the internal audits	Corrective and preventive action to address nonconformities
Preassessment	Registrar selected	Audit report
Corrective Action	Nonconformities raised during the preassessment	Corrective and preventive action to address nonconformities
Initial Assessment	BMS operational and organization ready for independent assessment	Audit report and recommendation for registration

Introduction ❶

Validation is the final phase in the project approach. Once the BMS infrastructure and the core business process model have been designed, developed, and implemented, it is necessary to validate the entire management system in order to determine whether it is both effective and compliant with any selected best-practice models such as ISO 9001. When a company has also elected to undergo an independent registration assessment, this phase also involves the registrar for the first time.

Starting Internal Quality Audits ❷

Using the skills and knowledge acquired during training earlier in the project, the project team (or designated quality auditors from elsewhere in the organization) must plan and conduct the first internal audits. Internal quality audits are at the heart of the continuous improvement system, together with the corrective action system and the higher-level management review, and play a vital role in validating the BMS. These audits provide a valuable health check at this stage of the project by helping the project team and management to:

✔ Gauge compliance to ISO 9001
✔ Help verify that the BMS has been effectively deployed
✔ Determine whether the BMS is effective
✔ Acquaint first-time internal auditors with audit techniques
✔ Raise staff awareness of quality across the company in readiness for external assessments later

Some companies elect to start internal quality audits as soon as parts of the BMS have been deployed. By auditing the BMS while it is being implemented, a company can begin to benefit from the controls and discipline imposed through the corrective action system. Even if a full internal audit is not appropriate until the validation phase, focused audits can begin much earlier in the project approach. For example a company can:

✔ Start auditing against the requirements of Document Control (4.5) early on
✔ Audit in production three months after the procedures and instructions have been deployed
✔ Ensure all staff possess training records and job descriptions (or equivalent)

The same principle is true for the management review process addressed in the preparation phase. All too often management reviews are not implemented until later in the project. This is counterproductive since the involvement of senior management during implementation is essential in overcoming obstacles such as a lack of support from staff or the project plan beginning to slip behind schedule.

Corrective Action ❸

The corrective action process provides the means to address any problems identified with the BMS. Across the BMS there are many different types of operational feedback that are fed into the corrective action system. As soon as the continuous improvement system has been implemented, a company can use corrective action to support implementation.

Relevant to the validation phase is the use of the corrective action system to address findings from both the first internal quality audit and the registrar's preassessment. The system ensures that any issues raised are addressed in a satisfactory and timely manner.

Preassessment ➍ ➎

Most companies undergo a preassessment audit about two or three months before the registrar's initial assessment. This preassessment acts as the final health check for the BMS.

Although almost all registrars offer this type of assessment, a registrar cannot offer advice or consulting after problems have been identified (accreditation precludes such a conflict of interest). Similarly, consultants performing a preassessment may not necessarily have the same interpretation of ISO 9001 requirements (or objectivity of the management system) as a registrar. For these reasons a company must decide whether the preassessment will be conduced by the registrar, by external consultants, or even by the internal audit team (although at this stage the internal auditors may not be sufficiently trained or experienced to provide the level of confidence desirable before the registrar's initial assessment).

In the same way the internal audit findings were addressed earlier, it is necessary to review the findings from the preassessment and implement effective corrective or preventive action. Particular attention should be paid to addressing any major nonconformities that could jeopardize the registration audit later in the validation phase.

It is worth noting that any assessments performed by the registrar (including a preassessment and initial assessment) should be included in the initial project plan as milestones. This is also true for the internal audit schedule, to avoid any duplication of attention toward the same processes or functions within the company.

Initial Assessment ➍

Once the company has achieved a stable and compliant BMS, the registrar can perform an independent initial assessment which, provided no major nonconformities have been found, will result in a recommendation for registration. Most registrars are satisfied by this stage with a corrective action plan showing how and when any nonconformities will be addressed, and they will issue a certificate on the strength of this plan.

In order to maintain the registration certificate, an organization will then have to undergo periodic surveillance (or *continuing assessment*) visits by the registrar. These audits typically occur twice a year, sometimes with a full reassessment after three years (*triennial reassessment*).

The first such continuing assessment visit will serve to verify that the findings from the initial assessment have been satisfactorily closed.

References

➊ Overview of Project Approach (A-1)
➋ Internal Quality Audits (C-2)
➌ Corrective and Preventive Action (C-1)
➍ Registrar Selection (T-3)
➎ Planning (A-4)

Preparation (A-2)

Which staff should comprise the project team, and how will they be trained? How will management ensure that these team members have sufficient authority with which to represent their functional area or processes?

What are the different audiences for project communication? For each audience, identify what communication vehicles already exist.

During the project, what ways can the Management Review meeting be used to support the project (over and above its role in reviewing the effectiveness of the management system itself)?

How will ownership of the management system be distributed throughout the organization? Is it possible to identify process owners for the major processes in the organization?

What statements of intent already exist (such as mission statements)? Does one of these policies act as a quality policy, demonstrating management's commitment to quality?

What are the selection criteria by which you will select a registrar? What weightings can be applied to each of these criteria based on management and project priorities?

Assessment (A-3)

Select a functional area within your organization and identify which elements of ISO 9001 apply to this area. Avoid including elements that apply to all functional areas (e.g., Management Responsibility and Control of Quality Records) which will become the management system infrastructure.

Outline a plan for conducting the diagnostic assessment in this same area, answering the following questions:

(a) Who will conduct the assessment?
(b) What preparation should they make before the assessment begins?
(c) Which staff should be interviewed?
(d) How long will the assessment take?

Planning (A-4)

What are the major risks that may impact the project? Outline a brief mitigation strategy to address each of these risks.

How will the project team be managed? What standard tools will the project team need?

Identify major milestones in the project and produce an early project schedule based on management's objectives for completion and/or registration.

BMS Design (A-5)

What factors should be addressed when investigating the following aspects of an organization:

(a) Culture?
(b) Technology?
(c) Organizational structure?

What parts of the management system provide the infrastructure to support all processes? How will these parts be developed and deployed early in the project?

Outline a possible structure for the quality system corresponding to the overall life-cycle of the organization and the infrastructure that supports it.

What are the types of document comprising this management system and their corresponding purposes? What tools and training must be provided to authors of these documents?

Process Deployment (A-6)

Map a simple process describing the way in which other processes within the organization can be analyzed, defined, and formally introduced into the management system. Address the role of the following ISO 9000 elements during this process:

(a) Document and Data Control (4.5)
(b) Quality System (4.2)
(c) Training (4.18)

Validation (A-7)

At which stage in the project can internal quality audits be started? Who will be trained as internal auditors?

How will the organization prepare for the registrar assessments (preassessments and/or initial assessments)? What training will staff need to understand the management system and be able to explain their involvement in this system?

ISO 9000
Management Systems

Project Toolkit

Generating Quality Awareness (T-1)
Establishing the Project Team (T-2)
Registrar Selection (T-3)
Understanding Processes (T-4)
Process Mapping (T-5)
Assessment Form (T-6)
Process Form (T-7)
Project Gantt Chart (T-8)
Organizational Environment (T-9)
Designing the BMS Infrastructure (T-10)
BMS Documentation (T-11)
Document Templates (T-12)
Process Libraries (T-13)
Managing Internal Interfaces (T-14)

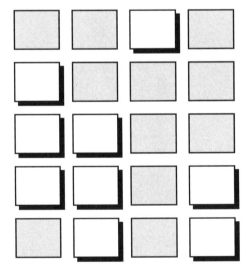

Introduction ❶ ❷

Generating and maintaining awareness and understanding of the project starts with the decision by senior management to implement quality concepts in the form of a formal management system. This awareness, however, is something that will need to be continued well after the project has been completed.

Although the project approach outlined here suggests starting to generate quality awareness prior to selecting a project team, some companies elect to establish the team first, and make such awareness a task of the project team. This usually causes the project team to become the focal point for project communications to the various different audiences. This is similar to the role expected of a quality function that tends to communicate with all functions within an organization, including customers and suppliers.

Effective communication during the project will dramatically increase its chances of success. Communication helps to overcome some of the pitfalls associated with change, especially since unless staff understand the need for change, such change may not have their active participation and support.

Producing a Communications Model

It is important for the project team to create a communications model (Figure T-1) early in the project. The role of the model is to help identify the different audiences that will require project communication. Each audience should be considered individually, since the type and volume of information will vary from audience to audience.

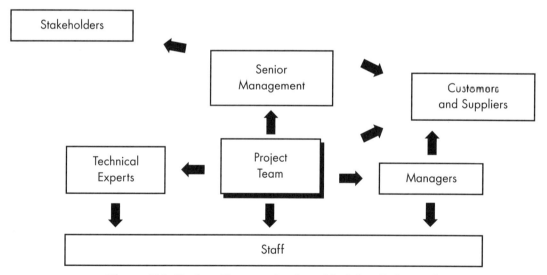

**Figure T-1: Project Communications Model to Raise and
Maintain Quality Awareness**

The model is useful in illustrating the different audiences for quality communications. Not only is project information provided (sometimes *cascaded*) to these audiences, but also note that there are arrows pointing back in the same direction that represent feedback and active participation of all audiences in the project.

Effective communication is required to disseminate all information, but particularly statements of direction and corporate intent. The communication is not just required within an organization, but also between an organization and its customers and suppliers. It is worth remembering here that significant changes to business practices through continuous improvement initiatives require thorough training within the organization, and often training for customers and/or suppliers.

Communication Plan

Based on the communication model and an understanding of the different target audiences, the project team will need to produce a communication plan. This plan identifies when and how project information will be shared with the organization. Early in the project, the information communicated will provide a general understanding of ISO 9001 and the project at hand. Toward the end of the project, the information will become more specific and will address such issues as the use of the management system and what to expect from the registrar's initial assessment. All the way through the project, results should be communicated so that staff can benefit from the project. For example, after the assessment, the project team will have collected valuable information on the processes within the organization that should be shared with staff involved with each process.

Depending on the type of information to be communicated and the audience, there are a number of different ways whereby the project team can communicate with the organization, for example, cascade meetings, all-hands meetings, staff meetings, and company newsletters.

Different Audiences

Stakeholders

In keeping with any improvement or change initiative within a company, this project should have the visible support and commitment of all stakeholders who, as appropriate, should receive background information on the strategic importance of quality management and plans for an integrated management system based on ISO 9001. Responsibility for communicating this information to all stakeholders usually falls on senior management.

Senior Management ❸

Typically, such awareness training is provided by external training organizations through either strategy sessions or management workshops. These sessions address topics such as:

✔ Background of quality management and standards such as ISO 9000
✔ Impact of quality management and ISO 9000 in their industry
✔ Features and benefits of ISO 9000
✔ Management systems (scope, purpose, structure, etc.)
✔ Overview of the project approach
✔ Project planning (including costs, timescales, milestones, resources, etc.)
✔ Role of management in the project

Whenever possible, these training sessions should make full use of case studies, exercises and group discussions to help reinforce understanding. Information packs should be distributed to attendees, including copies of the relevant factsheets from this Manual.

Managers ❹

Middle management will have a key role to play in the project. Not only are middle managers and supervisors often domain experts in their fields, they are responsible for cascading information down to their staff and providing feedback from staff to the project team.

Since the project will require the involvement of Technical Experts to assist the project team in developing formal processes, it is important for middle management to understand the importance of their commitment to provide adequate resources in their functional group or department. By providing Technical Experts, a manager can have confidence that the quality system will reflect actual practice and add value to the staff.

Communication between the project team and managers can take many forms, ranging from the active participation of these managers in a steering committee (to oversee the project) or the project team itself, through regular quality presentations by project team members during department or group meetings.

Technical Experts ❹ ❺

Technical Experts also have a critical role in the project through their active participation during process development. During this phase, Technical Experts assist the project team in its analysis and research of existing practices. Depending on the type of ownership model adopted, Technical Experts may also require some formal training in process analysis and mapping.

All Staff

Helping all staff to understand their role in quality and customer satisfaction is the responsibility of both senior management and the project team. In addition to managers cascading information to their staff, the project team can also provide awareness training directly to staff.

This staff awareness can be provided using short awareness sessions, information sheets with progress reports on the project, and articles in company newsletters.

References

    ❶ Preparation (A-2)
    ❷ Establishing the Project Team (T-2)
    ❸ Business Management Systems (B-3)
    ❹ Planning (A-4)
    ❺ Process Development (A-6)

Introduction ❶

The success of any large-scale project is largely dependent on the strength and experience of the project team formed to oversee the initiative, and the level of authority provided to them. A project of this type usually causes a significant impact on an organization, in terms not only of organization and processes, but also culture. It is essential that great care is taken in selecting the right project team to help facilitate this change. Successful change requires that the project team create awareness and understanding of the required change as well as coordinate the change itself: the introduction of formal processes.

To ensure the success of an ISO 9000 project, many factors have to be considered. Who will head the project? Who will make up the project team? What additional training will be required? This factsheet addresses these issues and helps build a profile of a successful project team.

Assigning a Project Leader ❷

To manage the project team and serve as liaison with senior management, a project leader is required. This individual may be the company's Quality Manager or VP of Quality, and must be in a position to discuss the project's strategic decisions with executive management. Management will need to carefully consider which individual member of staff is most suited in terms of qualifications, experience, and skills to have this responsibility.

ISO 9001 requires that the organization appoint a member of management who has sufficient authority to implement and maintain the BMS. Although it specifically allows the so-called *management representative* to have other responsibilities, to ensure its success, the implementation and maintenance of the BMS should be the individual's foremost responsibility.

Often the project has an ultimate member of senior management with the role of both **sponsor** and **champion,** who dedicates time and energy to provide active management visibility and involvement with the project.

Selecting the Project Team

The project team members should consist of staff drawn from all levels of the organization: senior management, middle management, product or project leaders, and supporting staff. This is important in gaining a good understanding of the organization from a number of perspectives. Team members should also be representative of all functional areas of the company; from departments such as engineering, manufacturing, and support activities (human resources, administration, etc.), even when their functions may directly fall outside the scope of certification. In the case of organizations spread over a number of geographic locations (such as sales offices, manufacturing locations, distribution centers, etc.), each location should be represented by a project team member. In addition there are specific skills that are required by the project team members, including:

✔ Management—good project management skills, team skills
✔ Personal—good communication and interpersonal skills
✔ Company knowledge—thorough understanding of the organization's structure, objectives, and culture
✔ Processes—multidisciplinary understanding of key processes and product lifecycles
✔ Technical—understanding of technical issues, product ranges, etc.

Preferably some team members will also have background knowledge or experience in quality assurance or quality control. However, such knowledge can be instilled through training.

Empowering the Project Team

It is estimated that over 70 percent of organizations are using self-managed or performance improvement teams. Results achieved by these teams can be as much as a 40 percent increase in productivity. However, the success of project teams depends on a number of issues, not least of all trust, leadership, and empowerment. The project leader must be empowered by senior management, and, in turn, must empower the team members by informing them of what to do and how to do it and then allowing them to do it. Empowerment is *not* delegation. In this context, it is more a process-focusing effort or energy in the direction of the project. Quality management is itself a powerful tool in building empowerment within an organization.

It is essential to ensure that both the project leader and individual team members are truly empowered to organize their work, and *not* forced to work within constraints that stifle creativity, in order to maximize the benefits of these teams. A team responsible for designing and implementing a BMS is no exception to this rule.

Training the Team ❸

A good understanding of quality management and best-practice models such as ISO 9000 is obviously critical for the project team (leader and members). Such knowledge is usually acquired by training and external support from consultants who act as facilitators and troubleshooters. All too often, however, companies send their project teams on an auditing course (three- or five-day) and expect them to be able to design and implement an effective management system. Such courses concentrate on auditing methods, and not the actual process of designing and implementing the BMS.

Instead, a different set of skills and knowledge is required by the project team in order to help guarantee the long-term success of the project. A suitable course would address everything discussed in the earlier sections, including:

✔ ISO 9000 and quality management
✔ Process concepts such as process analysis, mapping, and modeling
✔ Implementation skills including quality document development
✔ Internal quality auditing

Organizations sometimes train staff outside of the project team in internal auditing. This has a number of advantages in terms of raising awareness of quality management and capitalizing on the skills and knowledge base of the organization. It has the additional advantage of avoiding any future resource problems for internal audits.

When selecting a training provider, it is worth considering whether the courses can be conducted on site to avoid additional expenses. Most trainers provide this option, provided a minimum number of delegates attend the course. In the case of multisite organizations, the project team should consider whether this training should be centrally hosted or hosted at individual sites. It is also worth identifying a training company that can offer course material specific to your industry.

It is also beneficial for the project team to undergo a team-building course which, in addition to teaching valuable new skills to the team, can be used to establish a team charter and operating ground rules. The ground rules define how the team will operate in team meetings and how the decision-making process will work. Together with contact information for each team member, the ground rules can be published in a project team handbook that can be widely distributed.

Managing the Project Team ❹

A project of this kind is all-encompassing, taking in many functional areas and disciplines. Such projects can take up to 18 months to complete, and involve significant investment in internal (and sometimes external) resources. To help ensure the success of the project, it is necessary for both management and the project team to work within normal best-practice project management, such as review meetings of progress against milestones and regular progress appraisals.

Supporting the Project Team

In the same way that it is desirable that the project leader is dedicated to the project (or at least has limited other responsibilities), project team members should be able to dedicate sufficient time toward the project. Project team members do not tend to devote all their time to projects of this type, and will often maintain their current responsibilities while the quality system is introduced. At a minimum, team members can expect to spend between 40 and 60 percent of their time on the project.

In addition to training, there are other tools that can be provided to project teams to increase their effectiveness. For example, electronic mail systems can significantly increase communication and reduce the need for unnecessary meetings in order to exchange information and ideas. Sometimes, such teams never meet in person and are referred to as *virtual teams*.

Since up to 20 percent of an organization's workforce can be engaged in teams at any given moment, attention should be paid to the interfaces between this project team and other teams so that each team can leverage off the work of others. This is particularly true for organizations with multiple sites.

References

- ❶ Preparation (A-2)
- ❷ Management Representative (M-3)
- ❸ Internal Quality Auditing (C-2)
- ❹ Planning (A-4)

Introduction ❶ ❷

Many companies implement ISO 9000 with the objective of having their quality system **registered** or **certified** by a recognized third party at a later date. Registration offers a number of advantages to the company, not least of all a powerful marketing edge. It allows the company to use certification marks or logos on marketing material, thereby enabling a company to advertise its commitment to quality with demonstrated evidence through third-party assessment. Registration also allows the company to be listed in directories of ISO 9000 registered companies. Such directories allow purchasers worldwide to select companies with a proven commitment to quality in a given field or industry.

Registration is granted by **registrars** that are independent assessment bodies who assess companies against the ISO 9000 Standards (usually ISO 9001 or ISO 9002). There are over seventy registrars currently operating in the US, including several European registrars. Examples include Lloyd's Register Quality Assurance, BSI Quality Assurance, Kema, Underwriters Laboratory, National Standards Authority of Ireland, Inchcape Systems Registration, and Bureau Veritas Quality International.

Registrars are regularly audited by **accreditation agencies** that ensure that registrars are competent to operate in certain industries. In the US, the accreditation body is the Registrar Accreditation Board (RAB), which is under the auspices of the American National Standards Institute (ANSI) and the American Society for Quality Control (ASQC). In essence, accreditation helps to ensure that, for instance, a registrar with mainly textiles experience does not assess the engineering function of a software house.

Registration involves not only an **initial assessment** but **surveillance assessments** (sometimes called **continuing assessment visits**) for as long as the registration is maintained. For this reason, selecting a registrar (or certification body) is an important element of planning in preparation for your ISO 9000 registration. The objective is to establish a lasting partnership with a registrar that best meets both your long-term quality system *and* business needs.

Selection Process ❸

Although selecting the right registrar is very much a task for the individual company, this Manual includes an approach that is effective, irrespective of the company's industry and size (Figure T-2). Addressing these issues should help you ensure that the registrar you select will live up to your expectations and not prove to be a costly learning experience.

The selection process is usually started when the company is in the early stages of implementation (often during the preparation phase). This occurs for a variety of reasons; for example, some registrars are more helpful than others leading up to the assessment. Particularly in the case of companies experiencing pressure to obtain registration, it is also worth starting the selection process early to ensure that the registrar can accommodate any scheduling issues caused by lead times for assessment.

Invitation to Tender

The invitation to tender (**ITT**) document will help you make an informed decision as to which registrar best meets your business needs. It also serves to provide each registrar with the information necessary to scope the work and provide a quotation for assessment services (Tables T-1 and T-2). The ITT should be kept as brief as possible to ensure that it receives prompt attention, and a cut-off date should be set.

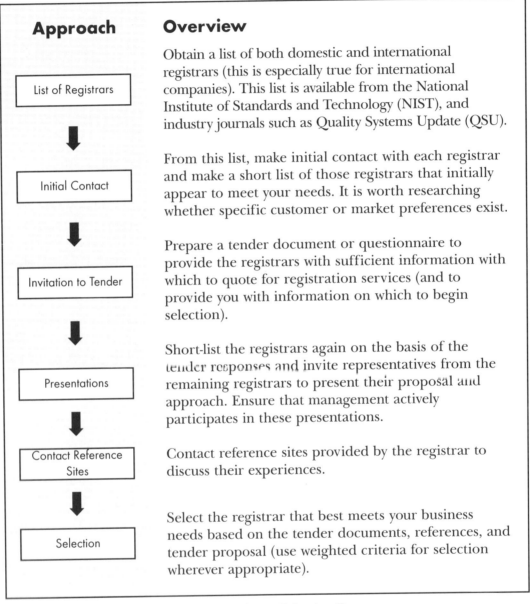

Approach

- List of Registrars
- Initial Contact
- Invitation to Tender
- Presentations
- Contact Reference Sites
- Selection

Overview

Obtain a list of both domestic and international registrars (this is especially true for international companies). This list is available from the National Institute of Standards and Technology (NIST), and industry journals such as Quality Systems Update (QSU).

From this list, make initial contact with each registrar and make a short list of those registrars that initially appear to meet your needs. It is worth researching whether specific customer or market preferences exist.

Prepare a tender document or questionnaire to provide the registrars with sufficient information with which to quote for registration services (and to provide you with information on which to begin selection).

Short-list the registrars again on the basis of the tender responses and invite representatives from the remaining registrars to present their proposal and approach. Ensure that management actively participates in these presentations.

Contact reference sites provided by the registrar to discuss their experiences.

Select the registrar that best meets your business needs based on the tender documents, references, and tender proposal (use weighted criteria for selection wherever appropriate).

Figure T-2: Registrar Selection Process

Section	Contents
Background Information	Provide marketing brochures, annual report, addresses, point of contact, product information, etc.
Organizational Structure	Provide an overview of how the organization is structured, with details on the number of staff at each location and the primary functions of each location where appropriate.
Scope of Registration	Define what products, services, and activities will be included in the initial assessment. The wording of the scope will ultimately become the wording on the registration certificate and accompanying directories of registered companies.
Specific Questions	See Table T-2 for specific questions to ask.

Table T-1: Framework for the Invitation to Tender (ITT) Document

Route to Registration

Once a registrar has been selected, the application process typically involves an organization making a formal application for registration services. At this point the registrar will provide you with the name of a client manager or lead assessor who will act as the point of contact leading up to the initial assessment (and sometimes beyond). Nearer this assessment, dates are agreed to between the organization and the registrar, and there is a documentation review to verify that the management system meets the requirements of the standard. This review tends to focus on the high-level documents within the system, such as the quality manual or business manual, and key procedures. Provided that no omissions are noted, the next step in the route to registration is the initial assessment audit or, in many cases, a preassessment.

Preassessment ❸ ❹

Some companies elect to have a preassessment prior to the initial assessment. The preassessment is essentially a trial run—a scaled-down assessment performed by the registrar or external consultants to determine a company's state of readiness for an initial assessment. The main purpose of a preassessment is to identify any issues that may result in failure during the initial assessment; these issues are known as major nonconformities. Before the initial assessment, a company must implement suitable corrective action to address these nonconformities. If a company opts for a preassessment, it is normally performed about three months before their initial assessment to allow suitable time for this corrective action. Both types of audit—preassessment and initial assessment—should be treated as significant milestones in the project plan.

Question	Explanation
Industry Experience	Can the registrar demonstrate the appropriate experience in your industry? What are the qualifications of the assessors? Can the auditors offer direct industry experience? What existing clients does the registrar have in your industry?
Accreditation	What accreditation does the registrar hold? Does their accreditation meet the needs of your international markets? Does the accreditation require a triennial reassessment? Can the registrar offer more than one accreditation through a single assessment? In the case of EU directives, is the registrar also a Notified Body?
Reputation	What kind of reputation does the registrar have in your industry? Who are their existing clients/your competitors? Seek reference sites and client lists. Are they respected for their attitude toward client care?
Market Share	What market share does the registrar hold, generally and in your industry? How many registrations has the registrar performed?
Locations	Where is the registrar headquartered? Does it have a local office? Will the auditors be flown in, or are they regionally based?
Proposed Approach	Who will be acting as client manager? Who will be the lead assessor and audit team members? Seek resumes of likely assessors and client managers and meet with them if possible. What sampling rate does the registrar use? In the case of multisite assessments, what proportion of sites will be visited?
Costs	What is the standard person day rate for assessments in your industry? Does this rate include local travel and subsistence? What are the travel costs (flights, etc.), including travel time? Is there an additional cost for document review or certificate issue? Is there an application fee and certificate fee? What is the cost of maintaining registration?
Reporting	What reporting mechanisms are employed? Does the registrar conduct opening, closing, and daily review meetings?
Surveillance Visits	What is the frequency of these audits? Will a triennial reassessment be required? What are the costs associated with certificate maintenance? Will there be consistency in auditors?
Individual Rules	Is the registrar bound by rigid contractual obligations such as charters or contracts? Does the nature of their accreditation impact on their services to clients (for example, special sector schemes)? Does the registrar impose any special requirements on its clients?

Table T-2: Questions to Ask in the Tender Document and Selection Process

Since accreditation precludes a registrar's offering consulting services, a preassessment provided by a registrar will not leave a company knowing what specific corrective action has to be undertaken before the initial assessment, just a report of nonconformities. However, it does serve to validate that a company has properly interpreted and applied the standard. Given the subjective nature of assessments and the disparity between interpretations, this benefit of the preassessment should not be overlooked. Another benefit of this approach is to help prepare staff in understanding what to expect when the registrar performs the initial assessment.

Preassessments are sometimes performed by external consultants who can mirror the registrar's preassessment approach while also recommending corrective action needed to remedy any findings.

References

❶ What Is ISO 9000? (B-5)
❷ Preparation (A-2)
❸ Validation (A-7)
❹ Planning (A-4)

Introduction ❶

Understanding processes is one of the key prerequisites in researching, developing, and implementing an effective quality management system. Often overlooked, process understanding can make a significant impact on quality management, which, after all, concerns process management and control. This factsheet addresses the fundamental principles behind process-driven organizations. It defines what a process is, and how to identify and analyze processes at varying levels of detail.

The most effective approach in designing and implementing a BMS is to focus on process-driven structures. This approach has many benefits discussed throughout the Manual, not the least of all that it encourages the breakdown of barriers between internal organizations such as departments or groups. Many processes have customer–supplier relationships that span several functions.

By focusing on processes, an organization can build a BMS that will help it become more responsive and flexible to change and improvement.

Understanding the Organization ❷ ❸ ❹

An organization centered around a **core business process model** which includes a number of **systems.** In the context of quality management, these systems represent a collective group of processes that interact together. Examples of systems include purchasing, design and development, and manufacturing. Systems also correspond to parts of the BMS infrastructure (such as the document control and continuous improvement systems).

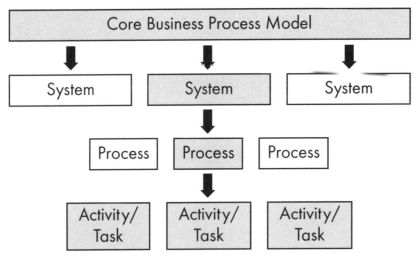

Figure T-3: Understanding How an Organization Works

Each system is comprised of individual **processes** that support the system. Using the example of a purchasing system, individual processes would normally address such activities as selecting new suppliers, the purchase order process, evaluating the performance of suppliers, and the maintenance of an approved vendor list (AVL).

A process, as this factsheet describes, is in turn made up of a series of smaller **activities** and **tasks** which, when performed in sequence, allow the completion of a process. Using the example of purchasing again, the process of selecting new vendors would include activities such as researching the industry to identify candidates, obtaining samples and background information on each candidate, and rating these candidates against certain selection criteria (cost, delivery, etc.).

These different levels of detail are reflected in the documentation found in the management system. For example, the core business process model is defined in the business manual, systems are described in guides, processes are defined in procedures, and activities or tasks are documented in instructions.

What Is a Process? ⑤

It is important to go back to basics and consider a simple process model, not just because process management is at the heart of quality management, but also because such a model helps to reinforce understanding of internal customer–supplier relationships (Figure T-4).

In this model, an internal supplier deploys resources to perform activities or tasks that convert these resources (input) into output of value to the customer (internal or external). Often such definitions talk of performance measurements and feedback loops that allow customers and suppliers to measure the effectiveness of their relationship and encourage continuous improvement. It is worth noting that within an individual operational interface, an internal organization may be acting as both internal customer and supplier.

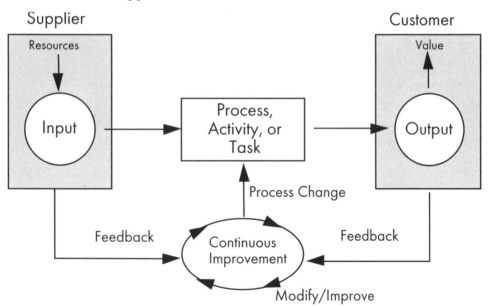

Figure T-4: Simple Process Model

Examples of resources deployed by the supplier include materials, procedures, information, staff, skills, knowledge, training, and plant or equipment. Examples of output include products, services, and information.

This view of a process is useful in identifying some of the core principles behind quality management. The concept of internal customers and suppliers can be applied to the interfaces and processes within an organization, not just with respect to external customers. ISO 9001 itself requires these interfaces to be carefully managed.

Through feedback from both supplier and customer, the effectiveness of the process is monitored through performance measurements, with process changes possible through continuous improvement.

Value Assessment

A common term associated with processes is value, which refers to the worth of the process output to both internal and external customers (Figure T-5). Studying the output from a process in terms of how this output is deployed by the customer allows the process to be classified.

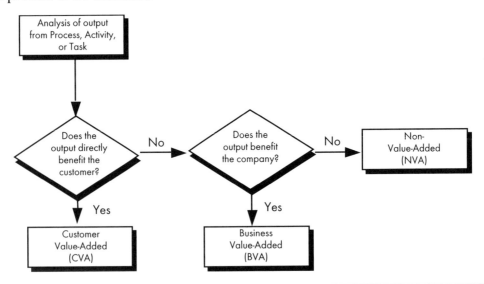

Objective	Explanation
Non-Value-Added (NVA)	Processes that do not add value to either the customer or the business as a whole. These processes may be redundant, in which case they can be removed to allow the streamlining of the process.
Customer Value-Added (CVA)	Processes such that ultimately the customer benefits from the output. When the external customer benefits from the process, CVA activities deserve special attention to ensure that customer requirements and expectations are being met (this represents the customer interface).
Business Value-Added (BVA)	Processes that benefit internal customers. These processes represent priorities for continuous improvement.

Figure T-5: Assessing Value Generated by a Process

Process Analysis ❻

Process analysis involves studying individual processes and systems as they relate to the overall core business process model. In addition to analyzing processes for value generation within the organization, there are a number of different factors that can be studied:

✔ Best-practice model compliance
✔ Processing and cycle time
✔ Operating/quality costs
✔ Frequency
✔ Volume
✔ Value assessment

Early in a company's experiences with quality management, process analysis is usually limited to a number of key factors, including compliance with best-practice models such as ISO 9001 and internal customer–supplier interfaces. As a company's management system matures and the company becomes experienced with process management and continuous improvement, it can start to analyze processes in more depth by considering additional factors.

References

❶ Assessment (A-3)
❷ Organizational Environment (T-9)
❸ ISO 9001 Roadmap (B-6)
❹ BMS Documentation (T-11)
❺ Managing Internal Interfaces (T-14)
❻ Process Mapping (T-5)

Introduction ❶

Understanding processes is critical to the successful implementation of formal systems and controls. Process analysis skills are important in gathering background information on a process. When it comes to describing the process, a process map graphically depicted as a flowchart enables the reader to instantly follow the flow events represented (Figure T-6). Flowcharts also greatly increase the user-friendliness of BMS documents such as procedures and instructions. Other benefits of using flowcharts include:

✔ Illustrating customer–supplier relationships where more than one functional group is involved with the process
✔ Providing a map that makes the identification of any redundancies or unnecessary loops easier, helping to identify non-value-added activities
✔ Enabling proposed changes to a process to be clearly illustrated and understood before change is implemented
✔ Identifying the interdependencies between different processes

Part of the training provided to project team members and process owners should include effective process mapping skills. The project leader should also consider the use of flowcharting software when mapping processes and producing BMS documents.

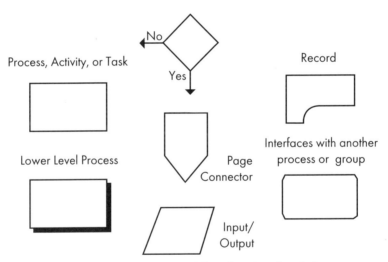

Figure T-6: Different Flowcharting Symbols

Flowcharting Applications ❷ ❸ ❹

Applications of flowcharting and process mapping can be seen throughout the implementation of a quality system. Even before work has begun on the BMS itself, process maps are used to understand an organization's core business process model.

Process maps are essential in understanding a process before that process can be defined and documented. Simple process models form the basis of interviews between team members and technical experts. Process flowcharts show a process broken down into individual activities, and are typically provided in BMS procedures. Lower down in the document hierarchy are instructions that break an activity into a series of tasks. Known as activity flowcharts, these flowcharts are provided in work instructions, the lowest level of detail within most business management systems.

Types of Flowcharting

There are two main types of flowcharting that are widely used when mapping processes: top-down flowcharts and Rummler-Brache flowcharts. Top-down flowcharts start at the top of each page and end at the bottom of the page when the process is complete. It is good practice to ensure that all the processes or activities within the flowchart are at the same level of detail. This helps to ensure that the flowchart is balanced. Where flowcharts do span more than one page, page separator symbols can be used. It is also helpful to use the symbols to describe the process or activity in active terms—verb followed by noun. For example, "raise change request" rather than "change request initiated."

The second type of process map commonly used in flowcharts is the Rummler-Brache method (Figure T-7). Such flowcharts are used to clearly illustrate the different parties involved in the process and their roles and responsibilities.

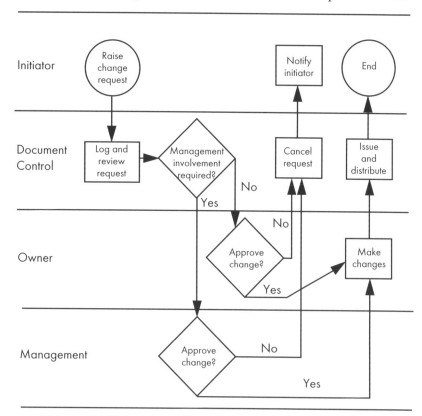

Figure T-7: Document Change Request (Rummler Brache)

References

❶ Understanding Processes (T-4)

❷ Assessment (A-3)

❸ Process Deployment (A-6)

❹ BMS Documentation (T-11)

1

Team Member

Date/Time
Interviewee
Ext./Room

Areas to be assessed

2

Describe the process within this area.

Summarize the individual processes.

Names of staff who could act as technical experts. **3**

Describe the types of record produced. Where are these records stored? **4**

What existing documentation is there? **5**

6

How does current practice in this area compare with the requirements of ISO 9001?

Applicable Elements

[ ]

[ ]

[ ]

[ ]

[ ]

7

List those individuals or groups that are affected by the process.

8

Summarize feedback from the technical expert on the project and, more specifically, the process. Are there opportunities for improvement?

Team Member

Date/Time
Technical Expert
Ext./Room

Process being researched

1

Describe the process. What activities or tasks are performed in the process (and in what order)?

2

Flowchart

Process entry criteria: When does the process begin?

3

Process inputs: What are the inputs into the process (resources, information, materials, etc.)?

4

Process exit criteria and outputs: When is the process finished or complete? What are the outputs from the process (information, products, deliverables, etc.)?

5

Process outputs: What are the outputs from the process (information, products, deliverables, etc.)?

6

Improvement Opportunities: Are there improvements that could be made to the process? If so, how would they change the process?

7

Notes

8

Phase	Activity	1	2	3	4	5	6	7	8	9	10	11	12
Preparation	Team Selection	▲											
	Mgmt. Presentation	▲											
	Team Training	▲—	▼										
	Registrar Selection		▲—	—	▼								
Assessment	Mapping Workshop		▲										
	Preparation		▲										
	Assessment			▲—	▼								
	Reporting				▲								
Planning	Data Collection				▲								
	Risk Assessment				▲								
	Planning Workshop					▲							
	Final Plan/schedule					▲							
BMS Design	High-Level Design					▲—	—	▼					
	Environment						▲—	—	▼				
	Cont. Improvement							▲—	▼				
	Management							▲—	▼				
Process Deployment	Processes 1-x					▲—	—	—	—	▼			
Validation	Mgmt. Review	▲		▲		▲		▲		▲		▲	
	Internal Audits								▲		▲		
	Preassessment											▲	
	Corrective Action											▲—	▼
	Initial Assessment												▲

Introduction ❶ ❷

There is a number of different perspectives on organizational structure. Once the foundations of an organization are understood, it is easier to understand why a management system must be process-driven (rather than driven by the elements of industry standards or organizational departments). This approach helps to avoid some of the pitfalls associated with implementing ISO 9001, and positions an organization well for continuous improvement and total quality management.

Quality Management and Organizations

Quality management is capable of achieving and supporting spectacular results in infrastructure, with organizations becoming much more flexible and better able to focus on meeting customer needs and expectations. The structure should focus on optimal customer service and consistently surpassing customer expectations.

Quality management represents the timely convergence of several new innovations and perspectives with the emphasis on business—and customer—value-added processes. It adopts both fresh strategies and established concepts to leverage core strengths and provide customer-driven solutions. It also allows for full use of accessible technologies and internal resources to define (and redefine) every aspect of how an organization works. For example, the focus may be capitalizing on new approaches to organizing and motivating people and evaluating supplier relationships.

Organizational Structure

The best way for an organization to view itself is as a system of integrated horizontal business processes supported by a number of internal factors. Typically, these factors are described as organizational, financial, and physical factors. Organizational factors relate to structure, management, processes, and systems. Financial factors refer to the financial controls over such factors as operating costs, budgeting, and financial reporting. Finally, physical factors include location, supporting transport, and distribution infrastructure.

To illustrate the principles of modern management thinking, an organization is said to be comprised of three elements: technology, people, and infrastructure (Figure T-8). In the context of the project, it is helpful to view an organization in this way. It helps to increase understanding of the importance of staff and resources, and the need for the management system (and the organization as a whole) to make best use of available technology.

Harnessing Technology

Harnessing available technology is a priority of all companies in this information technology age. The same is true with respect to a business management system that underpins core infrastructure components such as document management. Many organizations are now capitalizing on new technologies such as:

✔ Groupware, allowing for effective sharing of information and resources

✔ Client-server solutions, allowing access to technology and information to be distributed across the company

✔ Intranet technologies, allowing easy access to company information

In the context of a quality or business system, there are a number of software packages that help to implement and maintain formal procedures and records. Usually these applications concentrate in the area of document control, serving to ensure that only current and accurate documents are available for staff to use. Such systems also reduce the potential threat of obsolete documents being used.

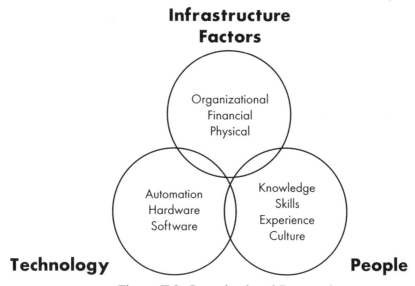

Figure T-8: Organizational Perspective

Some more specialized software packages provide further support in areas such as internal quality audit management and tracking corrective actions from identification of an issue through resolution. There are also modular packages that provide an integrated solution with other areas such as customer service, technical support, and product defects.

When considering the use of quality management software, it is important to first document your requirements, addressing issues such as compatibility of data with other packages (e.g., word processors and spreadsheets) and different computer platforms (e.g., Mac, PC, or Unix). Even when an organization has short-listed a number of packages that may meet its needs, it is always a valuable exercise to ask the vendor to arrange a site visit to another company or provide references for other companies that have an established system in operation.

Culture

Implementing a formal management system (such as the one proposed by ISO 9001) requires that management and the project team recognize the impact of the system on everyday activities of staff. Managing this transition and cultural shift in turn requires an understanding of softer issues such as communication and, more broadly, change management. A maturing of the quality system following implementation demands that the cultural shift continue, from early awareness of the importance of quality management, to more proactive ownership of the overall management system distributed across an organization. Heightened awareness of cultural issues is essential if the management system is to add incremental value within a company.

With operations becoming increasingly complex and the marketplace ever changing, a successful organization must harness the skills, experience, ideas, and knowledge of all staff. The best approach is to encourage teamwork, resulting in benefits such as:

✔ Breakdown of internal barriers
✔ Increased capacity for problem solving and troubleshooting
✔ Facilitated exchange of information, knowledge, and ideas
✔ Greater consensus of opinion with a higher chance of approval of the team's recommendations
✔ Cost-effective approach to projects

Organized and managed teamwork has the additional benefit of helping to create a more satisfying work environment, where morale is boosted as day-to-day issues are effectively addressed. The change in culture required of a company truly committed to quality encourages a move toward becoming a *learning organization,* one that encourages staff creativity, flair, and personal development.

Total quality management encourages motivation through participation in activities such as teams and quality circles. It also recognizes the need for an organization to instill a feeling of contribution, value, and worth among staff. Many of the concepts in this Manual offer insight into ways to encourage participation and empowerment of staff.

Contribution ought to be rewarded through recognition, which helps encourage the active involvement and commitment of staff. It can be a simple "thank you" and words of encouragement, or a more structured reward system linked to individual or team achievement.

Undergoing organizational improvement and change often encourages a company to reexamine its soul: *visions and values.* Conversely, studying company visions and values can result in organizational change, whether the change is manifested in cultural change, process improvement, or process innovation. Vision describes where a company is headed and its thoughts for the future. It is supported in turn by organizational objectives, mission statements, and other statements of intent. Values refer to the principles and beliefs that a company holds dear in its culture.

References

❶ BMS Design (A-5)
❷ Introduction (B-1)

Infrastructure Element	Comments	Factsheets
Document Control System	**Overview** Most nonconformities relate to document control in a management system. Care must be taken early in the project to establish an effective document control system that supports a document as it evolves from a draft to a released BMS document. Responsibilities can be shared between the process owner or author, those responsible for document control, and those affected by the process. **ISO 9001 Reference** Quality System (4.2) Document and Data Control (4.5) **Examples of BMS Documents** • Document Templates (Templates) • Documentation Standard (Standard) • Introduction to Document Management (Guide) • Producing a BMS Document (Procedure) • Implementing a BMS Document (Procedure) • Changing a BMS Document (Procedure) • Document Change Request (Form)	A-5, E-1, E-2, T-9, T-10, T-11 A-6
Records Management System	**Overview** Records provide objective evidence of the performance of the management system. Even with the best-designed BMS, a management system will not gain registration unless there are records to prove effective implementation. Records management should cater to both organization-wide recordkeeping (such as training records) and local recordkeeping (such as contracts). **ISO 9001 Reference** Control of Quality Records (4.16) **Examples of BMS Documents** • Managing Records (Procedure) • Archiving a Record (Procedure) • Company Recordkeeping Policy (Standard) • Master Record List (Template) • Departmental Record List (Template)	A-5, E-3

Infrastructure Element	Comments	Factsheets
Continuous Improvement System	**Overview** Designing and implementing the continuous improvement system is essential for the success of the management system. Each of the different types of improvement source should enter the corrective action system in a consistent way. Data from these sources should be summarized for the management review process. **ISO 9001 Reference** Corrective and Preventive Action (4.14) Internal Quality Audits (4.17) Control of Nonconforming Product (4.13) Statistical Techniques (4.20) Management Review (4.1.3) **Examples of BMS Documents** • Continuous Improvement Guide (Guide) • Preparing an Internal Audit (Procedure) • Conducting an Internal Audit (Procedure) • Internal Audit Checklist (Template) • Performance Report (Form) • Nonconforming Product (Procedure) • Concessions and Waivers (Procedure) • Applying Statistical Methods (Procedure) • Reporting Statistical Data (Procedure) • Management Review Process (Procedure)	A-5, C-1, C-2, C-3, C-4, M-5
Training Process	**Overview** Aspects relating to training and employee development are sometimes the most difficult to implement, not least of all due to the scale of a process that includes all staff. The training process can be integrated with job descriptions and the performance appraisal process. **ISO 9001 Reference** Training (4.18) Organization (4.1.2) **Examples of BMS Documents** • Employee Development (Guide) • Employee Training Process (Procedure) • Employee Training Record (Template) • Performance Appraisals (Procedure)	A-5, E-4, M-2

Introduction ❶ ❷ ❸

There are many different types of documentation within the management system, each of which requires a different level of control. The two main categories are process documentation and external documents (Figure T-9), both of which fall under document control. Additionally, there are many documents that fall outside of the management system per se, for example, a manager's memo, an internal report, budget information, etc. In these cases simple document control measures may be used (author, date, and pagination—n of N).

A number of quality records are generated as a result of processes described in BMS documents. Not to be confused with process or quality documentation, quality records provide objective evidence and operational feedback on a process and fall under strict controls, as defined in ISO 9001, clause 4.16, Control of Quality Records. Examples include design plans, technical specifications, engineering drawings, blueprints, audit reports, and job descriptions.

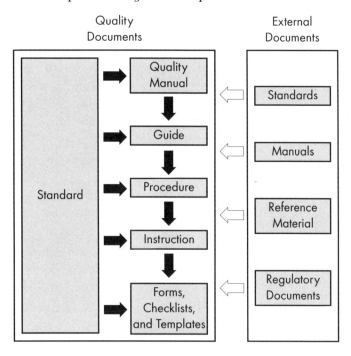

Type of Document	Explanation
BMS Documents	Elements of the BMS that describe how the organization operates. Also referred to as *process documents,* these documents make up the BMS documentation hierarchy and are auditable during internal audits and registrar assessments.
External Documents	Documents typically maintained by external organizations and used in a company as reference material.

Figure T-9: Types of BMS Document

BMS Document Hierarchy ❸

BMS documents are structured in a hierarchy according to the level of detail required by the reader (Figure T-10). Supported by a Business Manual, all systems within the infrastructure and core business process model should have a high-level introductory Guide (or roadmap) that provides an overview of the different processes within that system. The Guide is supported in turn by Procedures, each of which addresses an individual process within that system.

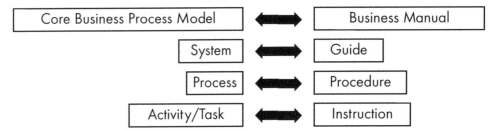

Figure T-10: Relationship Between Processes and BMS Documents

While Procedures contain requirements at a process level, Instructions provide specific information relating to how an individual activity is conducted as part of a process. Finally, Procedures and Instructions are supported by forms, checklists, and templates that capture process and product data. To illustrate the different levels of detail associated with the document hierarchy within the BMS, consider internal audits as an example.

BMS Document	Contents
Business Manual	High-level overview of the overall management of the internal audit program, illustrating how internal audits form an integral part of continuous improvement. Provides reference to the Guide.
Guide	High-level introduction to how internal audits are planned, scheduled, conducted, and reported. Provides references to individual procedures within the internal audit system (optional).
Procedures	Set of procedures addressing the processes for managing aspects of the internal audit system. Each procedure provides reference to individual Instructions.
Instruction	Depending on the level of detail in the procedures, Instructions provide specific task-by-task instruction to the reader. For example, a work instruction explains how to complete audit checklists.
Forms, Checklists, and Templates	Tools to support the reader in following either procedures or instructions. For example, annual audit plans, audit schedules, audit trail forms, nonconformity forms, corrective action requests, etc.
Reference Material	Standards such as the ISO 10011 series addressing Quality Auditing

Table T-3: Document Hierarchy for Internal Audit Process

Business Manual ❶ ❹ ❺

This document serves as a high-level introduction and roadmap to the BMS. Typically, the Business Manual is a policy document, demonstrating how the BMS supports each key business area in the company and each element of the quality system infrastructure.

The Business (or Quality) Manual serves a number of different purposes, including:

✔ Communicating the quality policy and other Statements of Intent
✔ Helping existing staff in understanding the BMS
✔ Quality training and awareness for new hires, contractors, and suppliers
✔ Presenting an overview of the BMS to customers to demonstrate the company's commitment to quality
✔ Demonstrating compliance with best-practice models such as ISO 9001

When companies intend to undergo an independent assessment of the quality system, it is important that the Manual illustrates that the BMS meets all the requirements of the standard. Many companies structure the Quality Manual (and in fact the BMS itself) around the requirements of ISO 9001. As the ISO 9001 Roadmap suggests, this does not provide a logical structure to ensure that readers will understand the BMS.

ISO 9001 (1994) recognizes that a Quality Manual can also take the form of a reference tool rather than simply a document existing for registration purposes.

Consistent with the philosophy of integrating business management and quality management, some companies create a **Business Manual** to serve the same purposes as a Quality Manual, yet ensure that the BMS is integrated with the business objectives and goals of the organization.

As ISO 9001 suggests, additional guidance is provided in ISO 10013, which also makes a useful differentiation between a *quality assurance manual* and a *quality management manual.* It describes a quality assurance manual as one that can be shown to customers and that does not contain any proprietary business information. A quality management manual may contain proprietary information, such as goals and objectives, and is not intended for use outside of the company. Consideration should be given before including any proprietary business information that may not be appropriate for an external audience.

Guides, Procedures, and Instructions ❸ ❹ ❻

BMS documents should be clear and concise, with no more words than are necessary. To encourage the use and understanding of processes, most organizations make wide use of flowcharts that enable the visual representation of activities. Note that at the lowest level, work instructions may be in the form of drawings and diagrams, depending on their application and intended audience.

Forms, Checklists, and Templates

In the day-to-day operational activities associated with the BMS, forms and checklists will be required to facilitate the capturing of process data. These quality documents fall under the document control system, and later become quality records. Examples of forms and checklists, continuing with the example of internal audits, include audit schedules, audit trails, and nonconformity forms.

Standards

Some companies also design and produce company standards as part of the BMS. Standards describe the internal standard for individual processes or issues. Standards outline the requirements in terms of policy and practice and tend not to discuss process approach, as such. An example of a standard is the house style and format of quality documents.

External Documents

Frequently the BMS is supported by additional information that is still under formal document control. These documents are usually revised and developed by national and international standards bodies or regulatory agencies. Reference material may also include material for other initiatives such as total quality management. Examples of such material include:

✔ Quality system standards such as the ISO 9000, ISO 9000-3, ISO 8402, etc.

✔ Regulatory directives and guidelines, for example the Food and Drug Administration's Good Manufacturing Practices

✔ Product conformity standards

In the case of standards, photocopies are not sufficient to satisfy registrars and Notified Bodies, since it is necessary to be able to demonstrate suitable control over external documents. The objective is to ensure that should an external document be revised, staff are made aware that older versions currently in use have been superseded.

Local Documentation

In many companies, a differentiation is made between centrally-controlled documentation and organizational (or local) documentation. An example of local documentation is detailed engineering instructions. It sometimes makes sense to impose a simple set of minimum document controls over these documents, but allow the engineering department to locally control them.

References

❶ Designing the BMS Infrastructure (T-10)

❷ Quality System (E-1)

❸ Understanding Processes (T-4)

❹ Document Templates (T-12) and Quality System (E-1)

❺ ISO 9001 Roadmap (B-6)

❻ Process Mapping (T-5)

Business Manual

Section	Contents
Cover Page	Provide document control details such as revision status, part number, approval authority, etc.
Contents	Contents page for quick reference.
Introduction	Explain the scope and purpose of the manual, and identify its intended audience.
Organizational Overview	Provide brief background of the organization—size, locations, products/services, etc. (include an organization chart).
Managing for Quality	Include statements of intent, compliance statements, management representative, and other quality management considerations. Summary of responsibilities relating to management and quality.
Management System Overview	Provide brief overview of how the management system is designed and structured.
Infrastructure	Describe the infrastructure components and explain how the infrastructure supports the entire BMS, for example, the document control system, records management, continuous improvement system, and training.
Product/Service Lifecycle	Describe the lifecycle showing how the different functional organizations interact. Explain each key process with a high-level description.
Supporting Activities	Describe the supporting activities such as purchasing, calibration, etc. Explain each key process with a high-level description.
Cross Reference Matrix	Provide a matrix that shows a comparison between: - the section in the Manual - the processes described in that section - guides or procedures that describe these processes - the applicable ISO 9001 clauses and subclauses - other industry or regulatory requirements, where appropriate.

Guide

Section	Contents
Cover Page	Provide document control details such as revision status, part number, approval authority, etc.
Scope	Describe how the system outlined in this guide fits with the management system (the guide does not contain requirements as such).
Purpose	Describe the purpose of the system in terms of output and value to the customer.
Related Documents	List all quality documents relevant to the system (such as procedures, instructions, and standards), and provide their reference or part numbers.
Definitions	Include brief definitions for terms introduced in this document.
Introduction	Provide an overview (with flowcharts) of the system and describe its relationship to other parts of the management system. Make reference to supporting Procedures where applicable.
Process Overview	Provide an overview (with flowcharts) of the process addressing at a high level the responsibilities, authorities, and interrelationships of those individuals involved with the process. Make reference to instructions and other procedures, where applicable.
Process Overview	Repeat for each process within the system.

Procedure

Section	Contents
Cover Page	Provide document control details such as revision status, part number, approval authority, etc.
Scope	Describe what processes are addressed by this procedure and which groups or departments are affected by its contents (the procedure contains requirements).
Purpose	Describe the purpose of the process in terms of output and value to the customer.
Related Documents	List all quality documents relevant to the process (such as procedures, instructions, and standards), and provide their reference or part numbers.
Definitions	Include brief definitions for terms introduced in this document.
Process	Provide an activity-by-activity overview (with flowcharts) of the process, addressing the responsibilities, authorities, and interrelationships of those positions involved with the process. Make reference to instructions and other procedures where applicable.
Records	List all records generated by following this process, and provide their location and retention period.
Performance Measurements	Identify any applicable performance measurements or metrics associated with the process.

Instruction

Section	Contents
Cover Page	Provide document control details such as revision status, part number, approval authority, etc.
Scope	Describe what activity is addressed by this instruction and which staff are affected by its contents (the instruction contains requirements).
Purpose	Describe the purpose of the activity in terms of output.
Process	Provide a task-by-task overview, using whatever format is appropriate for both the complexity of the task and its audience.

References

❶ BMS Design (A-5)

❷ BMS Documentation (T-11)

❸ Quality System (E-1)

❹ Understanding Processes (T-4)

❺ Document and Data Control (E-2)

Introduction ❶

Many management systems expect business pressures and the organization to remain constant. This tends not to be true in many industries, since internal and external pressures can often require a company to undergo rapid transformation or adaptation to processes and controls to meet new operational expectations.

Such adaptations can range from strategic repositioning or the introduction of new products or technologies, through subtle variations to the core product or service lifecycle (e.g., the series of processes or steps required to ship products or deliver a service).

The management system design proposed here not only supports this need for adaptation; it actively encourages it to help ensure that the BMS is always capable of supporting not just the quality management needs of an organization, but also the organization's business needs. It is built around a number of different concepts, including process libraries from which the BMS can call upon a suite of individual processes.

By calling upon different processes from the library, an organization can effectively customize or tailor its operational approach to support programs, projects, products, processes, or circumstances with very specific and individual needs. Examples of process library approaches can be seen in many industries, including the pharmaceutical, chemical, defense, and electronics industries. For example, Device Master Records can be used to apply specific map process documents (such as work instructions or specifications) to a device as it is developed and manufactured.

Need for Adaptation ❷

Process libraries can provide an organization with operational flexibility to deal with many **internal** and **external** factors or situations. For example:

✔ Customer contract requires a specific approach to either development or production which falls outside of the scope of the current quality system. In this instance, additional processes can be developed, implemented, and added to the library. The need to define the new approach or process flow can be met through the production of a quality plan (**external**).

✔ Variations to the lifecycle are sometimes required due to the diversity of either product or project. Some projects, for example, simply do not need the same degree of quality management and control as others. Typically, this is dependent on factors such as the criticality of the product or complexity of the project (**internal**).

✔ Variation in market requirements may force a company to explore new product opportunities requiring a rapid design and development approach (**external**).

Using Process Libraries ❸ ❹

Although the concept of process libraries forms a central part of the overall management system design, it serves a number of very specific applications that the flexibility and control of the library approach can support: activities such as quality planning (4.2.3) and development planning (4.4.2).

In the same way that a company maintains a document master list or quality record list, using process libraries requires a similar list—in this case, a library index that lists the different processes within a system (Figure T-11). For example, the design and development system will contain processes such as design reviews, testing, validation, and prototyping.

Similarly, the training process may include processes for managers reviewing their staff's need for training, and for the human resources department maintaining a training file for staff. These processes are listed in the index of forms in the process library.

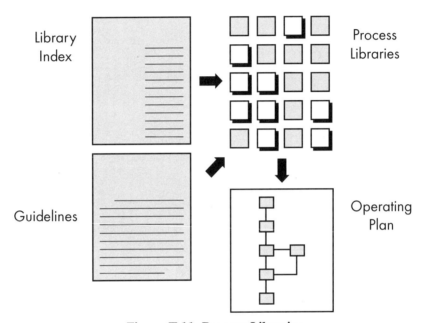

Figure T-11: Process Libraries

Managers and staff can determine an operating approach (such as a development project) by applying guidelines (provided in BMS guides and procedures). These guidelines provide selection criteria which help evaluate the operating approach based on applying the criteria dependent on internal or external pressures. Once the operating approach has been reviewed and approved by all groups or individuals affected by the process, it is documented in an operating plan, process-tailoring approach, or equivalent document.

Selection Criteria

For new programs, projects, or products (and even as a result of the need for a tailored approach to existing projects/products), the program manager must define the tailored process approach. Typically, this approach is defined in a project plan, operating plan, or equivalent, with guidelines and criteria defined in procedures. During the development of these procedures, the project team should work with program managers to define selection criteria for deciding which processes are required for that specific project.

Often a company will also ensure a minimum set of operating requirements that apply, irrespective of the type of project or product. These **mandatory** processes are defined in the guidelines and must, at a minimum, be compliant with any best-practice models being followed such as ISO 9001. Libraries will also contain a number of **optional** processes that apply under certain circumstances or perhaps for individual products.

These selection criteria are based on a number of factors, including:

✔ **Business pressures:** Pressures such as the desired time to market may impact on the selection process, provided that the approach does not compromise product quality.

✔ **Nature of the project:** Some smaller scale projects simply do not justify the controls exercised over a larger program (involving, for example, a number of subordinate projects).

✔ **Type of product:** Similarly, some simpler products require less by way of process control and verification/validation activities. The degree of process control should be commensurate with the criticality of the product (established during risk assessment within product planning early in the development process).

In addition to addressing such topics as scope, purpose, objectives, resources, and other typical planning details, the operating plan should describe the justification based on risk for the selected approach (which criteria were applied and in response to which pressures) and a detailed overview of the operating approach.

Following the selection process, the program manager and quality manager can review the operating plan for suitability, with the quality manager being included in the formal approval process for that document. It is during this approval cycle that other affected parties would be included in the approval of the operating plan.

Documenting the Process Libraries ➎

There are many ways to simplify both the selection of processes (defined in the guidelines) and also the subsequent documentation of operating approach (the operating plan). One such approach is shown in Figure T-12, in which flowcharting can be used to illustrate which processes are mandatory and which processes are currently documented within the management system.

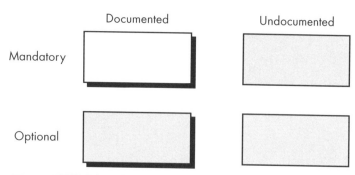

Figure T-12: Flowcharting Approach to Process Libraries

References

❶ BMS Design (A-5)

❷ Introduction (B-1)

❸ Design Control (L-2)

❹ Quality Planning (M-4)

❺ Process Mapping (T-5)

Introduction ❶ ❷ ❸

Section 4.3, the Contract Review clause of ISO 9001, refers not only to proposal and contract review activities with external customers and suppliers, but also to the relationships between internal customers and suppliers within an organization. Managing these interfaces is critical to the success of an organization since they have a direct impact not only on the effectiveness of business practices, but also on the quality of the end product or service. This is especially true for large companies whose many internal organizations interface and work together during the course of day-to-day activities.

Typically, the scope of registration in an ISO 9000 initiative is limited to the product or service lifecycle: that is, design and development through production and delivery of the product or service. While elements such as Training (4.18) touch upon internal functions such as a human resources department, often there are areas of an organization that fall outside the scope of a business management system (BMS). Rolling out the BMS to address these business areas becomes a key postregistration activity when companies turn their attention toward quality system maturity. In the meantime, these interfaces must be defined to fully satisfy the requirements of ISO 9001 and ISO 9002.

Process Model ❹

Before exploring the issues behind such interfaces, it is important to go back to basics and consider a simple process model, not just because process management is at the heart of quality management, but because such a model helps to reinforce understanding of these internal customer–supplier relationships.

In this model, an internal supplier deploys resources to perform activities or tasks that convert these resources (input) into output of value to the customer (internal or external). Often such definitions talk of performance measurements and feedback loops that allow customers and suppliers to measure the effectiveness of their relationship, and encourage continuous improvement. It is worth noting that within an individual operational interface, either internal organization may be acting as both internal customer and supplier.

Service Level Agreements

Many companies choose to define, manage, and control relationships between these internal organizations through the use of Service Level Agreements (SLA). An SLA is a formal agreement that defines all aspects of an operational interface. Such criteria include organizational charters, scope, responsibilities, point-of-contact, expectations, deliverables, process, exception handling, and performance measures.

An SLA is typically required where business practices or processes span two or more internal organizations, or where the absence of such a defined operational interface may adversely affect the quality of the product or service provided. Normally such SLA documents will not be required between product groups or their equivalent within the same internal organization.

Since SLA documents span different internal organizations, a single format for such documents may not be appropriate and may conflict with chosen format and style guidelines within different groups. For this reason a template providing a document structure, format, and content may prove useful in helping to ensure that individual SLA documents address the same criteria.

Interface Criteria

Although the particular details of an interface will vary from company to company and perhaps even within the same company, Table T-4 will act as a useful guideline for determining the interface criteria that should be addressed in an SLA document.

Content	Description
Charter	The individual charters of both customer and supplier should be stated in the SLA.
Scope	The scope of the SLA should be clearly defined and agreed to by both parties, and should make reference to the services provided by the supplier in the relationship. Similarly, if there are service areas that fall outside of the SLA, these areas should be specifically excluded in the scope to avoid possible misunderstandings.
Responsibilities	Both the customer and supplier should define the staff with ultimate responsibility for reviewing and approving the SLA. Typically, a member of management will have responsibility in this area.
Point-of-Contact	Both parties should define a single point-of-contact who is responsible for maintaining performance against the SLA.
Expectations	Service and product expectations of both parties should be clearly detailed and listed in each area as defined by the scope of the SLA. Note that these expectations typically include agreed-upon objective measurements such as timeliness of service, quality of deliverables, etc.
Deliverables	Deliverables between the parties should be clearly defined, including details of suitable review and approval controls (or other acceptance criteria) associated with each deliverable.
Process	Procedures and work instructions pertinent to this process or relationship should be referenced.
Constraints	Where appropriate, the SLA should define possible constraints on both parties that may affect the performance of the relationship.
Exception Handling	In the event that customer or supplier expectations are not adequately met, a dispute arises, or the nature of the relationship falls outside of the parameters of the SLA document, suitable exception handling and escalation processes should be defined.
Performance Monitoring	Frequency and nature of the performance reviews conducted between the customer and supplier.
Charges	Details of any charges associated with the services provided under the SLA.

Table T-4: Interface Criteria

Maintaining Records ➎

Any records generated from the SLA, such as the results of metrics and other performance monitoring measures, should be recorded, distributed to both parties, and stored at an appropriate location accessible to both parties. Both the nature of these records and their location should be specified in the SLA. Similarly, SLA documents themselves are quality records that require suitable control.

Auditing Internal Interfaces ➏

An effective SLA based on the interface criteria proposed in this section will automatically monitor the performance of an interface, helping to identify performance issues and introduce improvements. These improvements will often be assigned to the members of staff responsible for managing and maintaining the SLA. In the same way that actions arising from a management review meeting can be tracked in a corrective and preventive action log, actions relating to SLA performance review can also be managed through the continuous improvement system.

Internal auditing should also study these interface relationships, with audit trails leading into other internal organizations, as required. Both the use of SLAs and cross-functional auditing can be important first steps in breaking down internal barriers and moving to a more process-centric approach to quality management, rather than remaining constrained by a compliance model such as ISO 9000 or internal organizational structures. Where internal organizations fall outside of the scope of the quality system, audits can still be used to verify the effectiveness of the SLA by examining the supporting records. This is the approach that most registrars take when examining how an ISO 9000 quality system manages processes that involve organizations that are outside of the scope of registration.

References

➊ Organizational Environment (T-9)

➋ Designing the BMS Infrastructure (T-10)

➌ Contract Review (L-1)

➍ Understanding Processes (T-4)

➎ Control of Quality Records (E-3)

➏ Internal Quality Audits (C-2)

Generating Quality Awareness (T-1)

Who are the different audiences that the project team's communication model must reach?

At what stages of the project will information have to be communicated to these audiences?

What communication tools are at the project team's disposal (e.g. organization newsletters)?

What kind of training in the management system will all staff receive as processes are deployed?

Establishing the Project Team (T-2)

Who has the most appropriate skills, experience and leadership to lead the project team?

Which functions or groups will be represented on the project team?

How will this team be trained?

What resources will the project team need in order to ensure the success of the project?

Registrar Selection (T-3)

What benefits will the organization gain by undergoing an independent registrar assessment?

Considering what your organization does, what would the scope of registration be?

What your customers have any registrar or accreditation preference?

What qualities are you looking for in a registrar?

Understanding Processes (T-4) and Process Mapping (T-5)

Map out the core business process model within your organization, ending with the delivery of products or services to customers and any ongoing support activities.

For the process of raising a purchase requisition, identify the supplier, customer, process inputs and process outputs.

Produce a simple flowchart to represent the steps involved with that process.

Organizational Environment (T-9)

What technologies could be harnessed by the project?

Are there any cultural issues that the project team may encounter? How can management actively support any changes that the management system may bring?

How can teamwork be best encouraged during the project?

How will the project teams communicate, particularly between different locations?

BMS Documentation (T-11)

Outline a simple document hierarchy, briefly describing each type of document within the management system and its purpose.

What form will the Business Manual take? Who are the audiences of this Manual?

What different types of work instruction are needed across the company? Will any of these instructions be product or project specific?

What types of external document exist in the organization?

Process Libraries (T-13)

Are key processes in your organization tailored to particular projects or products?

What are the factors (internal and external) that require these processes to be flexible and adaptive?

What review and approval should this tailoring go through to ensure that minimum standards are always met, regardless of these factors?

How can the management system be built to promote and support process libraries?

Managing Internal Interfaces (T-14)

List the internal functions and departments that are excluded from the project but which act as internal customers or suppliers to the management system.

Addressing one of these interfaces, outline a simple service level agreement between the internal customer and supplier, defining the expectations of both parties.

ISO 9000
Management Systems

Environment

Quality System, 4.2.2 (E-1)
Document and Data Control, 4.5 (E-2)
Control of Quality Records, 4.16 (E-3)
Training, 4.18 (E-4)

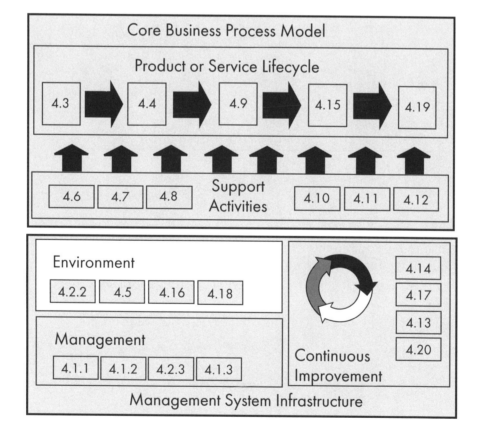

Overview ❶ ❷ ❸

In essence, this clause of the standard requires a company to implement a documented management system. It defines how such a system should be structured, with a quality manual or business manual supported by procedures (and work instructions). Typically a management system document hierarchy reflects the level of detail in the document, starting with the high-level quality manual or business manual and descending to the low-level detailed work instructions (Table E-1).

ISO 9001 makes the observation that the level of detail contained in the different types of document is determined in part by the skills and experience of staff and the complexity of the process. In other words, there is a balance to be sought between the detail provided in these documents and the qualifications, experience, training, and skills of staff.

Where staff are highly trained, there may be less cause for documented procedures and instructions. Conversely, a complex process may require more detailed documented procedures where staff skills and training are not sufficient to ensure process control. Striking this balance is one of the challenges of ISO 9000, in order to avoid unnecessary documentation and unwanted bureaucracy.

Level	Explanation
Quality Manual or Business Manual	Serves as a high-level guide to the management system. Typically the quality or business manual is a statement of intent or policy, demonstrating how each of the elements of the standard is addressed.
Procedures	Defines the next level of detail supporting a particular quality element. A procedure typically explains the process at a high level, but does not address individual activities or tasks that form a process. Each procedure references the relevant work instructions.
Work Instructions	Defines tasks or steps to take in order to follow a procedure and may take a variety of forms depending on their application.
Reference Material	Examples include standards addressing product conformity issues, guidelines, and any regulatory standards or directives.

Table E-1: Document Hierarchy

Documentation Required

✔ Quality Manual or Business Manual document, including the quality policy, presented as either a stand-alone document or a reference tool

✔ Procedures addressing each process within the management system, ensuring coverage of each element of the standard

✔ Work instructions for a specific and detailed task or activity defined in a procedure

Implementation Approach

✔ Examine any existing documentation for accuracy and compliance.

✔ Design the structure and "look and feel" of the management system.

✔ Document processes, ensuring coverage of each element of the standard.

Changes from ISO 9001 (1987)

✔ Now specifically requires a quality manual (or equivalent reference tool)

References

❶ BMS Design (A-5)

❷ BMS Documentation (T-11)

❸ Designing the BMS Infrastructure (T-10)

Overview ❶ ❷ ❸ ❹

The standard requires that all documentation within the management system be controlled. Documentation falls broadly into two categories: *product documentation* and *process documentation*, both of which fall under control. Examples of product documentation include drawings, specifications, blueprints, inspection and test results, and product or user guides.

Process documentation refers to documents within the management system itself, such as procedures, work instructions, and the business (or quality) manual.

The basic requirements addressing document control are that each document is accessible, approved, current (or at the correct revision in the case of historical documentation), and suitably stored. In addition, controlled documents must be distributed and managed in such a way as to ensure that obsolete (or out-of-date) product and management system documents are removed, destroyed, or marked as reference. As a guide, controlled documents would typically include the following level of control:

✔ Title
✔ Date of issue
✔ Document owner
✔ List of approval authorities
✔ Reference number or part number
✔ Revision
✔ Pagination
✔ Brief change history
✔ Distribution list

It is also necessary to establish and maintain a master list of controlled documents that identifies the current revision status of all documents. This list helps to avoid the use of obsolete and superseded documents. The most robust approach to the creation of a master list is to catalog all management system documentation but allow for segmentation of the lists in a logical manner to suit the company's needs (for example, departmental lists). On the other hand, product documentation may be cataloged by project or product type.

As the management system grows and opportunities for continuous improvement are found, changes will need to be made to procedures and other controlled documentation. This process is sometimes referred to as *up-revving* (i.e., releasing a new revision of a document). A similar process occurs for making engineering changes.

When document changes are made, the review and approval of the new version should be performed by the function or organization that performed the initial review (or someone with all of the necessary information and experience). Typically, departments or project teams either hold regular meetings to review any change requests or instill maintenance of these documents as a responsibility of document owners.

When making document changes, organizations should consider the effect that changes in one area may have on other parts of the organization or product.

Documents should be marked or stamped to demonstrate whether they are controlled or uncontrolled documents, current or obsolete. This is especially true in companies that use software solutions to manage their documentation. Although a document is always current on-line, as soon as it is printed, it is potentially obsolete and, as such, needs to be marked or stamped "For reference only."

The 1994 version now mentions documents of *external origin* that must also be treated as within the controlled system. Examples include customer specifications, national and international standards, and regulatory documents.

Documentation Required

✔ Documentation control procedures addressing document formatting, review, approval, release, and change processes
✔ Document change request form
✔ Change notice form
✔ Master list and master set of controlled documents

Implementation Approach

✔ List all documents within the management system, including quality records.
✔ Establish a company style for quality documentation.
✔ Verify review and approval methods for document issue and reissue.
✔ Establish and implement change control procedures.
✔ Use internal audits to increase discipline and understanding of document control.

Changes from ISO 9001 (1987)

✔ Refers to document and data control, since many companies use an on-line management system and electronic quality records
✔ References retention of documents or data for legal or other purposes

References

❶ BMS Design (A-5)
❷ Designing the BMS Infrastructure (T-10)
❸ BMS Documentation (T-11)
❹ Document Templates (T-12)

Overview ❶ ❷ ❸

Quality (or process) records demonstrate that desired product quality is being achieved, and that the process and the BMS are operating effectively. Objective quality records contain direct and indirect evidence that demonstrates whether the product or service meets specified requirements, and can sometimes be the only evidence of product quality. Equally, quality records reflect the level and depth of process control; quality records are generated during the operation of a process, and become the data repository for process results.

There is confusion about the use of this term; sometimes the BMS documents (quality manual, procedures, and work instructions) are referred to as *quality records*. However, this is inaccurate since the management system merely defines the system and process controls that manage the organization; it does not provide evidence of effectiveness. It is the quality records themselves that provide evidence of compliance against specified requirements or quality objectives. Considering the pyramid structure reflecting quality document hierarchy, quality records are an additional tier at the base of the management system, acting as a repository for collecting operational data (objective evidence) from the system.

Examples of quality records can be found across the entire organization. Almost all processes generate records, including:

✔ Technical design drawings
✔ Design or requirements specifications
✔ Operational sheets or checklists
✔ Test results
✔ Training records
✔ Internal quality audit reports

Sometimes organizations may be required to store and maintain selected quality records that relate to the quality of products for a specified part of the operating or product lifetime. A company should be in a position to provide this information and demonstrate adequate control and retention of such records.

ISO 9001 does not specify a minimum time period for retaining quality records. Although retaining records for five to seven years is common practice, registrars have varying opinions on the subject, and it is worthwhile seeking clarification on this issue to avoid any differences in opinion later in the implementation process. Provided a company can demonstrate that it has defined a retention period consistent with the nature of the quality records and any business or contract requirements, these problems should be avoided.

Organizations should also consider the following factors, which may have specified requirements relating to retention periods:

✔ Industry regulations and legislation (e.g., the Food and Drug Administration's Good Manufacturing Practices)
✔ Legal issues relating to product liability
✔ Product or operating life
✔ Individual contractual requirements with suppliers and customers

In addition to retention periods, the standard also requires that the following issues be addressed:

✔ Identification of all types of quality records, usually in the form of quality record indexes or a list of records associated with a process defined in a quality procedure
✔ Collection, filing, access, and suitable storage of all types of quality records
✔ Disposition and identification of obsolete or outdated quality records requiring removal from circulation

Contractual and regulatory issues can also sometimes dictate where or how quality records should be stored so as to avoid damage and deterioration. In the absence of such controls, common sense should be applied: fireproof safes are not necessarily appropriate in all instances! Again, provided an organization can demonstrate that the controls are sufficient and adequate, then compliance in this regard is not an issue.

The requirement for indexing of quality records is often misunderstood, although the principles behind a master document control list (4.5) can be readily applied to quality records. Typically, a central master record list is maintained that lists all types of quality records across the management system. This master list is supported by process or functional lists that provide the following additional information:

✔ Type of record and record name
✔ Procedure or work instruction with which the record is associated
✔ Medium (electronic form or paper-based record)
✔ Location
✔ Retention period

On-line management systems with electronic quality records have obvious advantages, not least of all real-time accuracy, control (read/write files, security, etc.), history, and immediate removal (or archiving) of obsolete documents. There are a number of software packages on the market to assist with the maintenance of BMS documentation and quality records.

Documentation Required

✔ Index of quality records showing location, authority, etc., for each type of quality record
✔ Quality records to demonstrate the effective operation of processes within the BMS

Implementation Approach

✔ List all types of existing quality records.

✔ Identify a list of quality records that will be required.

✔ For each record, address the following issues: identification, collection, indexing, filing, storage, maintenance, and disposal.

✔ Apply documentation and formatting controls to all quality records.

Changes from ISO 9001 (1987)

✔ Clarifies that quality records can take a variety of forms, including electronic records

References

❶ BMS Design (A-5)

❷ Designing the BMS Infrastructure (T-10)

❸ Document and Data Control (E-2)

Overview ❶ ❷

ISO 9001 recognizes the importance of training with this clause. It discusses the need for staff training across an organization in order that staff and the organization as a whole can achieve quality objectives. Appropriate training should be provided to all levels of staff that perform activities affecting quality.

This includes executive management, technical staff, engineers, process supervisors, administrative staff, staff in the field, and other operating personnel. In fact, it is generally agreed that *all* staff within an organization affect the overall quality of the products or services to customers.

A training process meeting the requirements of ISO 9001 should address the following issues:

✔ Evaluate the education and experience of all staff members, including both existing staff and new hires.

✔ Identify individual training needs for staff at defined intervals, usually in the form of a job appraisal or performance review.

✔ Provide appropriate training, internal or external, wherever necessary to ensure that staff can fulfill current and intended job responsibilities.

✔ Establish and maintain training plans and training records.

An organization needs to decide what is appropriate in terms of training, qualification, and experience for staff performing certain tasks and processes, and be able to provide objective evidence that staff members are suitable for these tasks. Experience may be substituted for education and training at the discretion of managers and supervisors. Sometimes industry regulations address the need for specific training requirements, and such requirements must also be addressed in the training process.

Consider, for example, process supervisors and operating personnel within a manufacturing process. Staff should receive thorough training (or be able to demonstrate suitable experience or qualifications) in the following areas:

✔ Operating instruments, tools, and equipment

✔ Safety issues relating to the work environment

✔ Certification or formal qualification required for any specialized skills

In this example, training needs would be identified typically through job reviews, and training needs documented and recorded in a training plan. Once training has been provided, details of the course or on-the-job training (OJT) would be recorded in the staff's training record, along with any other information, such as a certificate for successfully completing the training.

Such training records are required for all staff and should include the employee name and number, department and manager's name, date and duration of training taken (or training scheduled), and type of training received (name of course taken, OJT details, etc.).

Training records should be reevaluated periodically to help ensure that the training needs of staff continue to be identified and addressed. This normally takes place with performance appraisals between staff and managers. Often, the subject of training is closely linked to job descriptions (see 4.1.2), which usually prescribe the specific skills, training, and experience required for that position.

In addition to training on specific processes or skills required of staff, it is also necessary to train staff in quality matters, usually through awareness sessions. These sessions serve to communicate the quality policy to ensure that all staff understand the company's commitment to quality, and to introduce staff to the BMS. Issues such as navigating a management system, requesting a change to a process or procedure, and submitting an improvement suggestion should be addressed.

Often companies provide quality training to the project team, management, and internal auditors, but fail to recognize the need for all staff to be trained in the use of the management system. This becomes especially true when processes or activities have been changed or improved during the implementation of the management system. Similarly in the future, any significant changes to business practices should not only be controlled through the BMS, but also communicated to the staff impacted by the change. Neglecting this issue remains one of the reasons for failure during organizational change.

It is also worth considering that training may be necessary for suppliers and customers when process changes have an impact externally.

Documentation Required
✔ Procedures for recording, identifying, and providing training
✔ Training record and training plan template, completed for all staff

Implementation Approach
✔ Write a training procedure addressing the requirements of the clause.
✔ List all job functions and positions within the organization.
✔ Establish training requirements for each function, level, activity, etc.
✔ Prepare a training plan for each member of staff.
✔ Design a training record template to capture these training details.
✔ Complete training records for each member of staff.
✔ At defined intervals, review the training needs of staff.

References
❶ Designing the BMS Infrastructure (T-10)
❷ Organization (M-2)

Quality System (E-1)

What form of quality manual or business manual will best meet the needs of the organization while satisfying a registrar?

What are the different audiences of this manual?

What level of documentation is appropriate to reflect the skills, training, experience, and qualifications of staff?

Which staff are best placed to write the management system documentation?

Document and Data Control (E-2)

How should documentation for all functions be controlled?

Who is responsible for document control?

Where and when is documentation to be controlled?

Is there a distribution list of holders of controlled documents?

How are obsolete documents identified, stamped (or otherwise marked), and removed?

Control of Quality Records (E-3)

Where are existing records stored (e.g. centrally or locally)?

Who is responsible for maintaining these records? Are these records readily accessible?

Are retention periods defined and specified?

How are existing records, such as forms and checklists, managed under document control?

Do industry, customer, regulatory or other issues impact record keeping?

Training (E-4)

How are staff qualifications and experience currently verified?

What performance appraisal system exists already?

Does this system include the need to identify training needs of staff?

Are training records maintained for all staff?

ISO 9000
Management Systems

Management

Quality Policy, 4.1.1 (M-1)
Organization, 4.1.2 (M-2)
Management Representative, 4.1.2.3 (M-3)
Quality Planning, 4.2.3 (M-4)
Management Review, 4.1.3 (M-5)

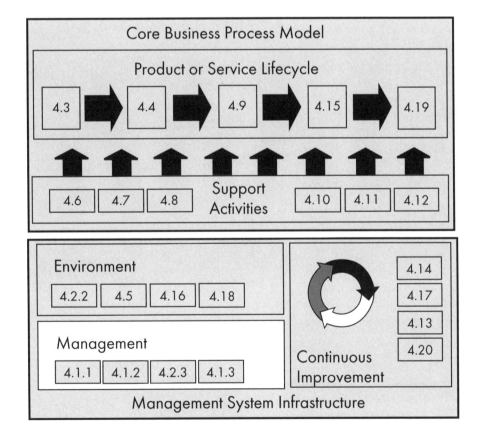

Overview ❶ ❷ ❸ ❹

Effective quality management begins at the top, with visible commitment and support to quality at an executive level. This commitment is made not only to an organization's staff, but also to its customers and suppliers. In the same way that a company usually has other *statements of intent* such as a mission statement, this element of the standard requires the organization to define and communicate a quality policy that addresses both quality management objectives *and* organizational goals. It follows that if quality management and business management are to become integrated, then the quality policy should be consistent with other business objectives and statements.

According to ISO 8402 (Quality Vocabulary), a quality policy is:

> The overall intention and direction of an organization with regard to quality, as formally expressed by top management ... the quality policy forms one element of the corporate policy and is authorized by top management.

The quality policy is defined, reviewed, and approved by senior management at an early stage of a quality management initiative, thereby helping to set the direction of the project. Such a policy should be easy for staff to understand and remember, relevant to the organization, and realistic (Figure M-1). It is not necessary for staff to remember the exact wording of the quality policy; however, the key messages and key words, at a minimum, should be known by staff throughout the organization.

Quality Policy

XIS is committed to committed to assisting our clients in
improving business performance through the provision
of innovative management consulting services and
products that consistently exceed our customer
expectations.

President & CEO
XIS Consulting, Inc.

Figure M-1: Quality Policy Example

There are many ways of communicating the quality policy to achieve this level of awareness, including:

✔ Including the quality policy in the quality or business manual

✔ Posting the quality policy across the organization, from the reception area to the different functional areas

✔ Reproducing the quality policy on corporate stationery or literature, or printing the quality policy on the back of business cards

✔ Including the quality policy on company trinkets such as drink mats, mouse pads, etc.

Remember that the quality policy should be signed by the President or Chief Executive Officer (CEO) and preferably the other members of executive management, and dated. This helps to reinforce to staff and customers the commitment of senior management to meeting quality management.

Once a quality policy has been established, documented, and communicated, it should be reviewed for continued adequacy and suitability by the management team. Usually, the Management Review is the forum for this.

Documentation Required

✔ Defined and approved quality policy

Implementation Approach

✔ Establish and define the quality policy at an executive level.

✔ Communicate the quality policy efficiently throughout the organization.

Changes from ISO 9001 (1987)

✔ Now requires the quality policy to reflect *organizational goals* and objectives

✔ Clarifies that the quality policy be established by executive management

References

❶ Preparation (A-2)

❷ BMS Documentation (T-11)

❸ Generating Quality Awareness (T-1)

❹ Management Review (M-5)

Overview ❶ ❷ ❸ ❹

This element of the standard requires that the roles, responsibilities, authorities, and interrelationships of all staff affecting quality be defined. It specifies quality-related activities as requiring special definition. However, it is commonly agreed that in fact all staff within an organization affect quality, indirectly or directly. Quality management addresses both internal and external customer/supplier relationships, demonstrated by the Contract Review clause (4.3) and the principles of Total Quality Management (TQM). Both reflect the need for all staff within an organization to understand their role in quality performance and, ultimately, in customer satisfaction.

Typically, a company will address these requirements by providing staff with job descriptions defining individual roles, responsibilities, and authorities. Most organizations use job descriptions extensively, since they form the basis of staff performance appraisals. Where generic job descriptions are used for a certain title or function, an individual's day-to-day activities should be documented or somehow defined with his or her manager or supervisor. Job descriptions are usually the responsibility of the human resources department, which tends to fall outside of the scope of most ISO 9000 initiatives.

Auditors tend to expect that staff will have copies of their job descriptions at their desk. Although this makes good business sense, it is not a requirement of the standard. Provided that staff are aware of their responsibilities and know where their job descriptions can be located, this is typically acceptable.

There are other ways in which staff roles and responsibilities can be defined without the need for job descriptions (Figure M-2). For example, management system documents such as procedures and instructions can be structured to allow clear definition of the staff member(s) responsible for performing a particular activity or step within a process. This proves to be a highly effective approach in defining roles and interfaces relating to a process.

6.1	**Submitting a Change Request**
Staff Member Appendix A	A member of staff who wishes to request a change to process document must complete a **Change Request Form** (FM126) and forward it to Document Control. Instructions on how to complete this form are given on the back of the form itself.
Document Owner Appendix B	Upon receiving the form and verifying that it is complete, Document Control prepares a **Change Notice** (FM134), defining the nature of the change, and forwards this pack to the Process Owner for attention.

Figure M-2: Assigning Responsibilities in BMS Documents

In meeting the needs of this element, an organization also needs to define and document its organizational structure. An outline of the overall organization structure is typically provided in the quality manual or business manual. This information may include an organization chart, an overview of the organization's departments and functional areas, and a description of the management structure. Such organizational issues can be discussed and monitored using the Management Review to ensure the currency of the information.

Staff must be able to demonstrate suitable training and/or experience in order to ensure that they can undertake their responsibilities effectively. In the case of quality, staff must have an awareness and understanding of quality, ISO 9000, and the use of the management system in their functional groups. This is accomplished through awareness training and communicating the quality policy to all levels of the organization.

To ensure the effectiveness of the management system and their commitment to its operation, it is imperative that management assign suitable resources to all quality activities, including internal quality audits. One of the roles of the Management Review is continuously to monitor the suitability of resources allocated to quality activities.

Documentation Required

✔ Job descriptions (or equivalent) for all staff with quality responsibilities clearly defined

✔ Overview of the organization and management structures in the quality manual or business manual

Implementation Approach

✔ Ensure that all staff understand their roles and responsibilities.

✔ Document these roles and responsibilities in job descriptions (or equivalent).

✔ Define the organizational structure in the quality manual or business manual.

✔ Ensure frequent review of resources to ensure adequacy for quality activities.

Changes from ISO 9001 (1987)

✔ Resources expanded to include management, work performance, and verification activities

References

❶ BMS Documentation (T-11)

❷ Management Review (M-5)

❸ Training (E-4)

❹ Generating Quality Awareness (T-1)

Overview ❶ ❷

A management system requires close control and management to ensure that all quality activities within the management system are effective and that quality objectives are being met successfully.

This element of the standard requires that the organization appoint a member of management who has the necessary responsibility and authority to implement and maintain the system. Although the standard specifically allows the Management Representative to have other responsibilities, quality management should be one of this person's foremost responsibilities to help ensure the effectiveness of the management system. There are exceptions, however, when perhaps the Management Representative is a member of executive management who delegates certain quality activities to, for example, a quality manager or project leader. In this instance, the Management Representative clearly has ultimate responsibility for overseeing the management system, but leaves its day-to-day management to another individual.

The approach taken to assigning responsibility for the management system varies greatly from company to company. This variation is due not only to the size of the organization and the availability of resources, but also to the commitment and understanding of senior management to the strategic importance of quality.

A quality manager who has sufficient responsibility and authority within the existing organizational structure can act as the Management Representative. Depending on the availability of resources and the size of the company, an organization that does not allocate a full-time owner is in danger of failing to capitalize on all of the internal benefits that it can provide.

The role of Management Representative requires that the individual possess a number of relevant skills and characteristics, including:

✔ Understanding of quality management and its critical importance
✔ Good communication, management, and interpersonal skills
✔ Support and attention of senior management
✔ Sufficient authority to ensure the success of the management system

Documentation Required

✔ Statement on the roles, responsibilities, and authorities of the Management Representative (usually in the form of a detailed job description and a short description in the quality manual or business manual)

Implementation Approach

✔ Define responsibility for the management system within the organization.
✔ Establish and document roles and responsibilities of the Management Representative.
✔ Ensure that the Management Representative has the visible support of senior management at all times.

Changes from ISO 9001 (1987)

✔ Requires the Management Representative to be part of senior management (sufficient authority to ensure that quality objectives will be met)

✔ States that the Management Representative may also be the primary point of contact with any third parties such as registrars

References

❶ Preparation (A-2)

❷ Establishing the Project Team (T 2)

Overview ❶ ❷ ❸ ❹

This clause was introduced in the 1994 revision of ISO 9001. According to ISO 9000-2, individual quality plans define how quality system requirements will be met in a specific contract, product, or project. For the purpose of discussion, this factsheet uses the word *project* to cover all such scenarios where a quality plan is required. The objective of a quality plan is to demonstrate how the quality of the project will be ensured throughout the design, development, production, and post-sales processes. Essentially it maps the project in question with the management system elements and processes. In the case of product development, for example, it also defines how the project or product will impact on the management system, and vice versa. In this context, a quality plan is an example of preventive action and business planning.

Sometimes built around the concept of process libraries or process tailoring, the quality plan or operating plan for a project may be a stand-alone document or, alternatively, a section within an overall project plan. The standard specifically states that one approach is to use a reference document that draws upon all of the integral management system documentation. A template can be used to capture this information and help ensure a consistent format across quality plans.

Such a quality plan should contain the following minimum information, or make reference to documents in which this data can be found:

✔ Quality objectives such as industry standards, product certification requirements and agency approvals, customer or contract requirements, etc.
✔ Defined requirements for each phase of the plan. This should include all requirements specifications, test equipment, production equipment, etc.
✔ Identification of all types of test, verification, and validation activities to be carried out. Any special types of test should be defined.
✔ Reference to resources with specific responsibilities for quality activities.

This type of quality plan can help make provision for new processes and controls, additional resources, new plant and equipment, and other requirements that will need to be addressed to ensure that the project can be effectively implemented.

Once a quality plan has been produced, it should be reviewed by all departments or groups involved in its implementation, including customers and suppliers, where necessary. Furthermore, the quality plan must be regularly reviewed and updated as defined in the overall project plan or business plan.

Another interpretation of quality planning refers to the management system itself rather than individual products, processes, or projects. By virtue of the fact that the system will evolve as the organization grows and changes, it is good practice to develop a medium- to long-term quality plan for the future growth and objectives relating to the quality system. After all, ISO 9000 implementation addresses a set of minimum quality management best-practice requirements, and provides only the foundation on which to build a world-class quality system.

In keeping with other quality records, all quality plans should be controlled documents that are accessible to (and approved by) the appropriate staff.

Documentation Required

✔ BMS documents addressing the development, release, and maintenance of quality plans

✔ Templates for quality plans

✔ Current quality plans for individual products, projects, and contracts (wherever appropriate)

Implementation Approach

✔ Identify and list the different types of plans across the company.

✔ Establish templates and guidelines for when quality planning is required, what individual plans should address, the approval of these plans, and their maintenance after release.

✔ Produce quality plans for all recent or new products and projects.

✔ Hold regular reviews to update these quality plans.

References

❶ Process Libraries (T-13)

❷ Design Control (L-2)

❸ Process Control (L-3)

❹ Planning (A-4)

Overview ❶ ❷ ❸

The management review provides a continuous review of the performance of the management system to help ensure its continued effectiveness and compliance. The review is closely associated with the continuous improvement system (Figure M-3) addressed in a number of the ISO 9001 elements.

Although the standard does not specify at which level this review must occur, it does make reference to *executive management,* and it is generally accepted that senior management should conduct the review. ISO 9001 refers to management with executive responsibility *for quality.* Whichever standard an organization adopts as a quality management model, it should be remembered that quality management must start at an executive level, with visible support and commitment demonstrated across the organization. With this in mind, an organization must decide what is appropriate both to comply with the model *and* maximize the business value of the review.

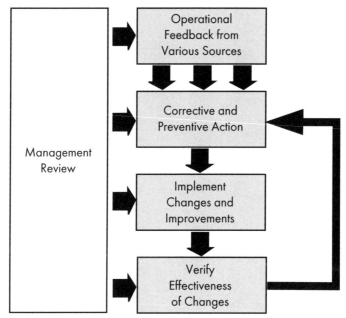

**Figure M-3: Role of the Management Review in
Continuous Improvement**

The frequency of management reviews is not specified and depends on the individual circumstances of an organization and the relative stability of the management system. During implementation, the frequency is generally higher (weekly or monthly) than it is once the management system has been both implemented and subject to regular internal quality audits (quarterly). Unfortunately, most companies do not conduct management reviews during implementation, thereby missing an opportunity to strengthen management support for the initiative.

The scope of reviews should be defined. Organizations often use template agendas to ensure that the management reviews address all the necessary topics, and to instill a sense of structure in the meetings. It is good practice to distribute any reference information to the management team prior to the review. Examples include quality reports, customer satisfaction reports, supplier reports, corrective action status reports, and information supporting any key issues to be covered during the meeting.

A management review should address (but not be limited to) the following topics:

✔ Actions from last review
✔ Status of organizational structure, particularly the impact of proposed changes to the BMS
✔ Continued adequacy of quality policy, objectives, and any other statements of intent
✔ Performance of the management system against organizational goals and the quality policy
✔ Achieved quality of product or service against customer expectations, internal conformance requirements, and any applicable agency or regulatory requirements
✔ Customer satisfaction (feedback, complaints, etc.)
✔ Supplier performance issues
✔ Internal quality audit and registrar audit findings
✔ Status of the corrective action system (open and closed issues)
✔ Process performance feedback from capability studies and metrics/measurements
✔ Adequacy of internal resources assigned to quality management
✔ Review of existing quality plans and identification of any new areas requiring quality planning or preventive action
✔ Issues requiring escalation, conflict resolution, or discussion

Issues should be thoroughly reviewed, analyzed, and resolved, with any designated actions clearly recorded. Actions should be addressed in a timely manner after the review, in keeping with the requirements of the corrective action system. It is necessary for records to be maintained of these reviews, usually in the form of detailed meeting minutes and supporting reports.

When companies are implementing a management system, they often ask customers and suppliers to come and present or discuss their ISO 9000 and quality experiences as a part of the management review. This has several benefits, not least of all closer quality management relationships and increased focus, as well as the opportunity for some informal benchmarking.

Documentation Required

✔ Records of management reviews (meeting minutes, etc.)
✔ Monthly reports on quality issues (where appropriate)
✔ Explanation of how these reviews interface with both the internal quality audit and corrective/preventive action processes
✔ Agenda template for covering topics

Implementation Approach

✔ Establish a management review team to analyze BMS feedback and confirm dates in advance.

✔ Design and implement a comprehensive, documented corrective action mechanism that addresses all types of feedback on BMS effectiveness and that provides the management reviewers with performance data.

✔ Ensure that summary reports of quality management issues are fed from the corrective action system into the management reviews.

Changes from ISO 9001 (1987)

✔ Standard now specifies that senior or executive (quality) management be involved in the reviews

✔ Requires that the management review occur at defined intervals and against quality policy and objectives

References

❶ Corrective and Preventive Action (C-1)

❷ Organization (M-2)

❸ Internal Quality Audits (C-2)

Quality Policy (M-1)

What are your organizational goals, and how do they interact with quality objectives and policy?

What other statements of intent exist, and where are they defined?

How can the quality policy be communicated throughout the company?

Organization (M-2)

Where is the organization structure currently defined?

Where are staff roles and responsibilities defined? Are staff always aware of their roles and responsibilities?

Can staff demonstrate the appropriate qualifications, experience, skills, and/or training to perform their responsibilities?

Do staff understand their role in quality?

Are adequate resources being assigned to quality activities such as internal quality auditing?

Management Representative (M-3)

Has senior management assigned an individual with sufficient authority to implement and maintain the management system? What are this individual's responsibilities?

Does this individual possess the necessary skills and knowledge?

Will the visibility of this individual demonstrate to all staff within the organization that executive management is committed to the management system?

Quality Planning (M-4)

Are quality plans being used by management for activities such as development planning and production planning?

Is quality planning an integral part of both business planning and contract review?

What should a quality plan address to maximize its use and value as a management tool?

Management Review (M-5)

How does management know if the management system is working effectively?

What management members ought to play a part in the Management Review process?

What are the quality and performance objectives against which the management system will be reviewed?

What aspects of the management system's performance should be considered as part of the Management Review?

How does management currently review quality issues, such as trends in customer satisfaction and product failures/defects?

ISO 9000
Management Systems

Continuous Improvement

Corrective and Preventive Action, 4.14 (C-1)
Internal Quality Audits, 4.17 (C-2)
Control of Nonconforming Product, 4.13 (C-3)
Statistical Techniques, 4.20 (C-4)

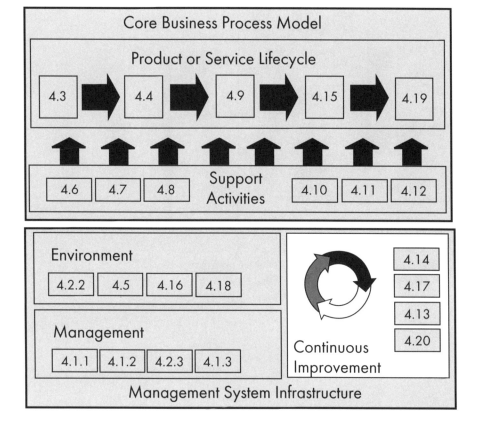

Overview ❶ ❷ ❸ ❹ ❺

The corrective and preventive action element is pivotal in ensuring the continued effectiveness of the management system and its conformance with both internal requirements (such as quality plans and objectives) and external requirements (such as ISO 9000). The 1994 version of the standard now specifically addresses preventive action. This helps to increase understanding of the difference between corrective and preventive action, consistent with the need to move toward *prevention* rather than *detection* (one of the many philosophies behind effective quality management).

Corrective action is directed toward the elimination of the causes of *actual* nonconformity found within an organization, for example, action based on any nonconformities found during an internal quality audit. **Preventive action,** on the other hand, is directed toward the elimination of the causes of *potential* nonconformities, for example, measuring the defect rates associated with products or services. It follows that as the management system matures following implementation, there should be a visible downward trend in corrective action and a marked increase in preventive action measures.

The combination of Control of Nonconforming Product (4.13), Statistical Techniques (4.20), and Internal Quality Audits (4.17), corrective and preventive action form the basis of the continuous improvement system (Figure C-1). This is also the vehicle whereby the management system can migrate from a reactive-based system to a proactive management system capable of sustaining the benefits of effective quality management and improvement strategies.

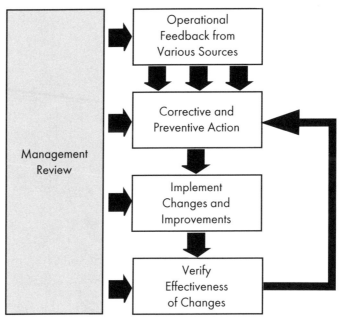

**Figure C-1: Role of Corrective and Preventive Action in the
Continuous Improvement System**

Taking operational feedback from sources such as internal audits and metrics, a problem can be analyzed and appropriate remedial action planned and implemented. Once this action has been deployed, it is later verified to ensure that it is effective in addressing the problem. The performance of the corrective and preventive action system is itself monitored on an ongoing basis through the management review process (4.1.3).

The main requirement of the clause is that a company establish and maintain a documented continuous improvement system capable of implementing corrective and preventive action, and take measures to ensure its effectiveness. It is necessary to record any subsequent changes to the BMS: changes to processes, procedures, and work practices.

ISO 9001 requires that corrective and preventive actions are appropriate to the magnitude of the problem or nonconformance, and this tends to imply that a risk assessment will sometimes be necessary to determine the severity of the issue before any action is agreed to or implemented. Problems affecting quality should be evaluated in terms of their actual or potential impact on such aspects as processing costs, quality-related costs, product characteristics (performance, reliability, safety, etc.), and, ultimately, customer satisfaction.

Analysis of nonconformities and issues should make full use of all available operational data such as the examples given below. Typically the corrective action system is built only to support the findings of the internal audit program, but fails to capture all types of feedback available from the management system, including:

✔ Internal quality audit results (findings and observations)

✔ Registrar audit results (preassessment, initial or surveillance assessment findings, and observations)

✔ Quality records (e.g., inspection and test records)

✔ Product defects and problems

✔ Supplier performance issues (e.g., material defects or delivery issues)

✔ Process monitoring data from capability studies or process analysis

✔ Customer complaints and commendations

✔ Improvement suggestions and opportunities for process improvement

Most companies analyze these issues at a local level to help identify trends that may indicate a deeper issue that needs to be addressed. Once a trend has been identified, it is entered into the corrective action system. By the same token, there may be individual instances of nonconformity that warrant direct entry into the system on the strength of their individual importance or severity. Such filtering helps to prevent the corrective action system from buckling under the strain of minor issues that can be addressed locally (Figure C-2). However, care should also be taken to ensure that such data is collected and logged in case a trend becomes apparent in the future.

Taking customer complaints as an example, a monthly report may be produced by the customer services manager and forwarded to Management Review for discussion. The report summarizes complaints received and actions taken, and flags any emerging trends. Any significant individual complaints are also reported, and are addressed directly through the corrective action system as appropriate.

Filtering provides a useful source of summary information to management, and is often facilitated through the use of statistical tools that help analyze the data and form conclusions. Examples of statistical techniques and tools include control charts, Pareto diagrams, and histograms. Such tools need not be complicated and often prove invaluable in interpreting data.

Once an issue enters the corrective action system for resolution, it is added to a corrective action log that allows the issue to be tracked through the system. This log captures all relevant data relating to the issue, such as:

✔ Originator and date the issue was raised
✔ Source of the issue
✔ Target date for completion of corrective action
✔ Actual date the issue was addressed
✔ Open/Closed (to show clearly which issues have yet to be resolved)

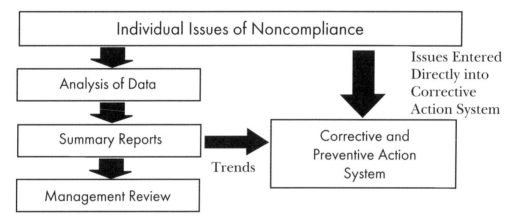

Figure C-2: Local Filtering

Although there are many software packages that provide automated corrective action systems, a simple spreadsheet can be used effectively as a log. Naturally, reports generated from this log should be among the reports discussed during the Management Review.

The next step in the corrective action process involves assigning an owner to address the issue. The owner may be the process owner, an internal auditor, a member of staff who raised the issue, or even a cross-functional task team in the case of more complex issues. It is then the responsibility of the designated owner(s) to determine all possible courses of action that will address the issue satisfactorily.

It is critical to try to identify and eliminate the real cause of the problem rather than compromise with a "patch" that may only address the issue temporarily. Statistical process control is often applied at this stage to conduct root-cause analysis of the problem. For example, cause and effect diagrams help to determine the deep-rooted causes behind the issue.

In some cases, a number of different actions may be identified as a result of this analysis. In order to select the most appropriate course of action, it is necessary to compare the individual solutions against *design performance criteria* and the current process. Such criteria may include cost, speed, use of internal resources, ease of implementation, and a simple cost-benefit analysis. This selection process enables the owner or task team to reduce the number of options based on these criteria until only one course of action remains, providing the most effective solution to the issue.

With the corrective action agreed upon, it is then necessary to produce an implementation plan (depending on the nature of the intended course of action). If, for example, a new process is required, the plan would address the need for quality documentation and any training or staff awareness deemed necessary.

Regardless of the nature of the action taken to address the issue or nonconformance, it is necessary to review this action at a later date in order to confirm that the action was effective and suitable. Typically, this is addressed using internal quality audits (and specifically the use of audit checklists).

However, there is also a number of alternatives, including:

✔ Using product, process, or system metrics
✔ Measuring the cost of quality
✔ Process capability studies

Often the weakest part of a continuous improvement system, some corrective and preventive action processes are designed only to address the immediate problem, but not to avoid its reoccurrence. Another common problem is that they often deal only with matters relating to the product or service, while overlooking the effectiveness of the overall management system itself.

Preventive action is largely overlooked by companies since it is not always fully understood. Preventive action is essentially the process whereby potential or possible issues are raised *before* occurrence. This generally involves some form of process analysis or capability study to determine where process problems are likely to occur in the future. Quality planning is a form of preventive action, since one of its roles is to identify areas where the BMS may not be suitable in its present form to meet the future needs of the organization. Trend analysis is another good example of preventive action. A number of minor issues or observations may indicate a growing trend in performance-related issues. By analyzing operational feedback and identifying trends, an organization has the opportunity to correct or improve the process or system before noncompliance occurs.

Continuous improvement is not always achieved through preventive measures identified through corrective action. A process is often proactively reviewed to achieve improved efficiency and effectiveness; this review is typically conducted by the process owner. For example, to introduce a measurable improvement to a process, it may be redesigned or reengineered to realize significant improvements. In this sense, continuous improvement introduces stable, incremental improvements, whereas the redesign (sometimes starting with a clean sheet of paper) achieves more dramatic results in performance. This is an example of preventive action that is not the result of corrective action; it is proactive rather than reactive.

Documentation Required

✔ Corrective and preventive action procedures integrating with other elements of the continuous improvement system

✔ Form to request corrective action and changes to the management system (typically referred to as a Corrective Action Request, or CAR)

✔ Log to track status of corrective actions until closure

Implementation Approach

✔ Design and document procedures for analyzing available operational feedback, identifying nonconformities (actual and potential), determining action required, implementing that action, and reviewing its effectiveness.

✔ Procedures should integrate with the other elements, such as Management Review and product nonconformances.

✔ Measure the effectiveness of corrective and preventive action through internal quality audits or other means, such as metrics.

Changes from ISO 9001 (1987)

✔ Includes a new section specifically addressing the need for preventive action

✔ Requires that corrective and preventive action be appropriate to the scale of the problem

References

❶ Designing the BMS Infrastructure (T-10)

❷ Management Review (M-5)

❸ Internal Quality Audits (C-2)

❹ Control of Nonconforming Product (C-3)

❺ Statistical Techniques (C-4)

Overview ❶

Scope and Purpose ❷

The purpose of an internal quality audit is to validate that the management system is working effectively and according to plans and objectives. Performed by trained auditors independent of the area being assessed, the internal audits review the compliance of processes to ISO 9000, the compliance of staff in following these processes in day-to-day activities, and the general health of the management system. Audit findings provide a valuable source of feedback to drive continuous improvement, with management getting visibility of the results.

In addition to audits as part of a schedule covering all processes and functional areas, internal audits may also be initiated for other reasons, including the following:

✔ A customer contract specifies an assessment or audit of some form.

✔ There are known problems or concerns with a particular project, process, system, or function.

✔ They verify that prior corrective and preventive actions were effective and appropriate.

Establishing an Internal Audit Function

Companies use very different approaches to establish an internal audit function. Depending on the size of the company, these range from a dedicated, central auditing team to trained auditor resources spread across the organization.

The internal audit manager (who is often also the management representative) is responsible for maintaining the internal audit plan and managing individual audits. Close links are needed between those staff responsible for internal auditing and those managing the corrective action system, to ensure the effective flow of feedback into the continuous improvement system.

Internal Auditors ❸ ❹

The basic requirements for internal auditors include an understanding of quality management concepts, an understanding of ISO 9000, and a good working knowledge of the company's management system. In addition, auditors must be trained to make effective use of audit techniques such as audit trails and audit checklists. Finally, auditors must have strong communication skills and an appropriate level of understanding of the area being audited so as to add maximum value to the audit.

Considering the Organization (4.1.2.2) and Training (4.18) elements, it is not clear whether internal auditors have to receive audit training from an external company in order to demonstrate that they have the appropriate level of knowledge and experience. It may be possible to use on-the-job training (OJT) internally, with more seasoned auditors providing the training during internal audits.

There remains the additional requirement that auditors be independent of the area being audited. There are several different approaches to meeting this requirement and resourcing internal audits in general. Some companies use cross-functional auditing, whereas others maintain a core team of independent internal auditors.

It is important that internal auditors be selected from as many different parts of the organization as possible. Suitable candidates are those staff who have a good understanding of the company and its products, but don't necessarily have direct QA experience. Since the project team should be multidisciplinary and representative of all internal functional groups and key process areas, project team members often become internal auditors. Either way, training must be provided to auditors, usually through an internal quality auditing training course. Such courses cover the use of audit trails across an organization, designing checklists, and effective communication skills.

Audit Planning and Scheduling

ISO 9001 requires a planned, systematic, and ongoing schedule of internal quality audits to ensure that the management is effectively implemented and that corrective and preventive actions are taken in a timely manner. This audit plan typically covers all functional areas, all clauses of ISO 9001, and a representative number of projects or products. In all cases, suitable sampling rates should be employed to ensure maximum coverage of the organization with the resources available (typically 25 to 30 percent of staff). It is normal to expect that every area will be audited at least once a year, with areas that produce audit concerns receiving more frequent scrutiny.

The internal audit plan, usually spanning a year, also has to address the use of internal auditor resources and the integration of any known registrar or supplier visits.

Audit Preparation

Prior to a scheduled audit, the audit manager or lead auditor coordinates the preparation. Issues to be addressed include notifying departments when the audits will be (helping to guarantee management and staff availability) and distribution of background information to auditors. This information may include:

✔ Copies of BMS documents that have changed since the previous audit
✔ Audit checklist forms (allowing an auditor to prepare questions for an interview)
✔ Audit trail forms (capturing data when an audit spans more than one functional area)
✔ Nonconformity reports (NCRs) or Performance Report Templates (PRTs)

Audit planning involves each auditor preparing an audit checklist for an assigned area. This checklist is used by auditors to prepare questions and map out a plan for what processes or projects to cover, and how. Usually it is helpful to schedule interviews with staff in advance. Internal audit interviews generally last about one hour each.

Conducting the Audit

Audits start with opening meetings where the audit team can confirm aspects such as the audit scope and schedule of interviews with staff and managers. In many respects an internal audit is similar in approach to the assessment performed earlier in the project.

At the end of each day of the audit, internal auditors meet to discuss their findings and reevaluate audit strategy. Often, trends become apparent when the auditors are presented with the opportunity to compare findings. For example, isolated obsolete procedures in one function may be simply a local discipline issue, whereas if the issue were epidemic across a number of different functions, it may suggest a broken process for removing obsolete documents.

During the audit, each auditor documents the audit trail taken (an effective audit follows a path wherever necessary across different functional groups or processes). The documented audit trail often proves useful after the audit has finished and the time comes to document more detailed audit findings. Auditors should also list all documents reviewed as a part of the audit, including such details as the revision status of each document. As part of the audit, the auditor can compare this list with the master document list to verify whether each document reviewed was the most current.

At the end of the final day of the audit, the lead auditor will collect the findings from each auditor, and summarize these findings in a closing meeting with management. This meeting helps to give management early visibility of results.

Recording Findings ❺

The findings from an audit fall into two broad categories: observations and nonconformities. Observations are used when either the severity of the issue does not warrant a nonconformity or the auditor wishes to bring attention to an opportunity for improvement. Nonconformities, on the other hand, refer to shortcomings within the management system that will need to be addressed. Such nonconformities can fall into two groups:

✔ **Major nonconformity:** An element of the standard has not been addressed, or there is a total breakdown of a process within the overall management system. A major nonconformity may also result from an accumulation of minor nonconformities raised against one functional group or one element of the standard.

✔ **Minor nonconformity:** There is a single lapse in the management system, either because it does not reflect actual practice, staff are not following the procedures and work instructions, or a specific requirement of ISO 9001 is not being adequately addressed.

All such findings are typically captured by auditors on a nonconformity report (NCR). Provided it is accepted as appropriate to enter the corrective action system, the NCR becomes a corrective action request (CAR) and enters the corrective action system. To stress the added value of internal audits in providing both positive and negative feedback on the effectiveness of the BMS, some companies now use Performance Reports that allow for different types of findings (not just nonconformities), including observations and improvement suggestions. A Performance Report Template (PRT) enters the corrective action system in the same way that NCRs enter the system.

Presenting Results ❻

After the closing meeting and the end of the audit, all reports and completed NCRs or PRTs are summarized into a report that is presented to management as part of the management review process. This report addresses the nature of the findings (nonconformities and improvement opportunities), successes, and failures of the audit.

Although senior management will not necessarily need to see copies of individual findings, managers and supervisors of areas covered in the audit need to see these findings to help ensure that corrective or preventive action occurs to remedy the issues. A copy of the report, together with copies of these individual findings, provides them with the information to understand how effectively the management system is operating within their area.

Documentation Required

✔ Auditing procedures addressing the interface with management reviews and the corrective and preventive action system

✔ Audit trail, checklist, and Nonconformity Reports (NCRs) or Performance Report Templates (PRTs)

✔ Internal audit schedule

Implementation Approach

✔ Select and train auditors and design the audit process.

✔ Identify the areas to be audited and produce an internal audit schedule.

✔ Conduct an initial quality audit to evaluate the adequacy of procedures.

Changes from ISO 9001 (1987)

✔ Requires that auditors be independent of those who have direct responsibility for the activity being audited

✔ Reinforces the role of internal audits in verifying corrective actions, and the interface between internal audits and management review

References

❶ Designing the BMS Infrastructure (T-10)

❷ Contract Review (L-1)

❸ Organization (M-2)

❹ Training (E-4)

❺ Corrective and Preventive Action (C-1)

❻ Management Review (M-5)

Overview ❶ ❷ ❸ ❹

A nonconforming product or service is one that fails to meet defined specifications or is at risk of failure to meet specified requirements. This term applies to product that occurs during the company's own processes as well as nonconforming product received by the supplier. In managing and controlling nonconforming product, it is necessary to address the following:

✔ Identify which products are involved in the nonconformity
✔ Document and evaluate the nonconformity
✔ Propose alternatives for disposing of the nonconforming product
✔ Physically control its movement and processing
✔ Notify all functions that may be affected by the nonconformity

Nonconforming product or material is identified through inspection and testing, from receipt of materials (receiving inspection), through the production or manufacturing processes, to final inspection before shipment or delivery to the customer.

Essentially, incidents of nonconformance should be documented using nonconformity reports (NCRs) or equivalent. Based on the nature of the defect or shortcoming, available data and inspection results should be evaluated to determine whether any further testing or inspection may be necessary. The standard stresses the need for nonconforming product to be segregated to avoid inadvertent use, with its inspection status clearly marked (4.12).

ISO 9001 requires that the responsibility for review and authority for the disposition of nonconforming product be defined. Considering ISO 9004-1, the individual responsible for review should possess the necessary experience in further processing, performance, reliability, and safety. Many companies use a **materials review board** (MRB) to address nonconforming product issues relating to products from suppliers.

The standard also offers a number of alternatives for nonconforming product. For each of these options, processes for disposition, notification, and classification of nonconforming products need to be defined. Similarly, processes for reinspection of repairs or rework are also required, as is a concession reporting and handling procedure.

Feedback associated with nonconforming product is one of the many inputs into the continuous improvement system. Although individual instances of nonconformity tend not to enter the corrective action system, such data should be collected and analyzed not only in order to determine the root cause of the problem, but also to help establish any trends or patterns in data. If a trend is highlighted, it suggests the need for corrective or preventive action, and under these conditions would enter the corrective action system directly. In keeping with the generation of local reports for each of the continuous improvement inputs, a report summarizing nonconformance activities is typically provided for discussion in the management review.

Although not specifically referred to in the standard, it is worth considering processes for addressing *situation management* as it relates to the overall management system itself. Typically, this would cover concessions, waivers, exception handling, and escalation approaches. For example, a project may not warrant the full controls exercised by the management system. One option for managing this deviation is the use of a quality plan that defines and justifies deviations from the norm. In the absence of a quality plan, it is still necessary to document the deviation through a concession or waiver that is suitably reviewed and approved. Escalation and exception handling are sometimes covered by the management review process.

Documentation Required

✔ Documented procedures addressing the identification through disposition of nonconforming product

✔ Operational forms and work instructions needed to record nonconformances

✔ Procedure addressing concessions, waivers, etc.

Implementation Approach

✔ Review current processes for the identification, documentation, evaluation, segregation, and prevention of inadvertent use or installation of products that fail to meet specifications.

✔ Ensure that procedures interface with Corrective and Preventive Action (4.14) and other elements of the continuous improvement system.

References

❶ Corrective and Preventive Action (C-1)

❷ Inspection and Testing (S-4)

❸ Inspection and Test Status (S-6)

❹ Management Review (M-5)

Overview ❶ ❷ ❸

The use of statistical techniques is often overlooked and poorly understood by organizations implementing a formal management system. This element of ISO 9001 addresses the use of statistical techniques and quality metrics as valuable tools associated with process management and verification activities. In fact, statistical techniques can provide the means whereby operational feedback relating to products, processes, *and* systems can be collected, analyzed, and applied toward continuous improvement.

With respect to products, statistical techniques include such activities as the use of statistical methods during inspection and testing to study variation in a product's characteristics compared with specified requirements. Other areas where statistical techniques may be applied to a product include:

✔ Market research studies
✔ Failure mode and effect analysis
✔ Regression analysis
✔ Test and acceptance criteria

Often the results arising from such statistical methods can be used to demonstrate conformance to quality requirements in a contractual situation.

Part of the confusion behind this element of the standard is that it is believed that the scope of statistical techniques is solely limited to product or service issues. **Statistical process control** (SPC) methods are widely used for measuring process capability, and similar tools can play a part in helping to analyze feedback relating to the management system. Taking continuous improvement as an example, the corrective action system is most effective when it involves root-cause analysis to determine the actual cause of an issue or problem. In this sense, the use of statistical techniques is an important aspect of the continuous improvement system. Other quality tools such as benchmarking make extensive use of statistical tools.

Irrespective of the application of statistical techniques, the requirements of this element of the standard address the need for close control and management in the following areas:

✔ Identifying the need for statistical techniques
✔ Ensuring the effective application of statistics through the use of documented procedures and guidelines
✔ Making provision for staff training in the use of statistical techniques

Documentation Required

✔ Documented procedures addressing the use of statistical techniques

Implementation Approach

✔ Identify existing statistical applications and controls.

✔ Design processes to address the use of statistical techniques across the organization.

✔ Provide training in statistical methods to staff.

Changes from ISO 9001 (1987)

✔ Requires an organization to establish the *need* for statistical techniques

✔ Requires that the use of statistical techniques is controlled through procedures and training

References

❶ Corrective and Preventive Action (C-1)

❷ Inspection and Testing (S-4)

❸ Understanding Processes (T-4)

Corrective and Preventive Action (C-1)

What examples of corrective and preventive action exist?

Who has responsibility to analyze product or process issues for improvements?

How does corrective and preventive action interface with internal quality audits?

What processes exist for follow-up when problems are found?

How is the effectiveness of action measured and verified?

Internal Quality Audits (C-2)

Are there frequent reviews of processes and systems for effectiveness?

Which staff should be trained as auditors and how will their independence be guaranteed?

Who will manage the internal audit planning?

What will happen to the audit findings and reports?

Control of Nonconforming Material (C-3)

Who has the authority to "sentence" non-conforming material?

How is this review and identification conducted?

What are the options for dispositioning nonconforming material?

How is such material segregated and identified?

Statistical Techniques (C-4)

What statistical techniques are used currently?

Are staff using statistics suitably trained?

Which activities require or would benefit from statistical analysis?

ISO 9000
Management Systems

Product/ Service Lifecycle

Contract Review, 4.3 (L-1)
Design Control, 4.4 (L-2)
Process Control, 4.9 (L-3)
Handling, Storage, Packaging, Preservation, and Delivery, 4.15 (L-4)
Servicing, 4.19 (L-5)

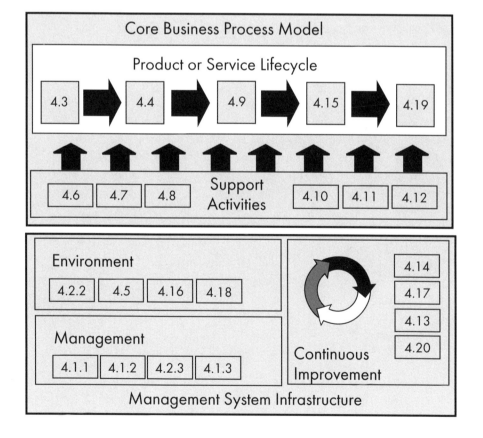

Overview ❶ ❷

Contract review addresses the issue of contracts (and the process for managing them) and their importance in understanding and meeting the needs of the customer. A factor that is often overlooked is the need to address both external customers and *internal* customers; in both cases requirements and expectations must be defined.

There are three main requirements in the clause that must be addressed:

✔ Customer contract or tender requirements are thoroughly defined and documented.

✔ Any changes to a contract are resolved, agreed to, and communicated to all parties affected by the change.

✔ The company can meet the defined requirements of the contract, order, or other statement of requirements.

Over and above ISO 9001, these requirements represent good business practices. To avoid potential misunderstandings between the supplier and the customer, all requirements should be defined and agreed to by both parties and properly documented.

This element specifically refers to verbal orders for products or services when a formal contract may not exist between the customer and supplier. These requirements must be defined in an appropriate way and validated by the customer.

Where an amendment to a contract occurs, it is necessary to resolve and agree to the changes with the customer, define the new requirements, and communicate these changes to those individuals or departments affected by the change. For example, a change in product specification may result from discussions between the marketing department, the purchasing department, and the customer. If these changes are not communicated to the design department, the product will not meet the customer's specification or requirements.

Contract review principles also apply to internal customer–supplier "contracts." When an interface exists between functional groups or departments, there is an operational understanding of the relationship by both parties. However, it is rarely formally defined in terms of the expectations of both parties to the interface. Consequently, it is often difficult to analyze the effectiveness of the relationship. This understanding may take a variety of forms depending on the formality of the interface:

✔ Verbal agreement or minutes of a meeting
✔ Procedure or other documented process
✔ Service level agreement (SLA) between the parties

In all these cases, the expectations of both internal supplier and customer should be defined, together with performance measures to gauge how effectively the interface is operating.

Documentation Required

✔ Documented processes addressing contract review activities with customers (internal and external)

✔ Template for service level agreements (where the organization is complex with many interfaces to define)

Implementation Approach

✔ Review current practice and compare with the contract review activities outlined in this element of ISO 9001, addressing any changes necessary for compliance.

✔ Identify and define internal customer–supplier relationships.

Changes from ISO 9001 (1987)

✔ Inclusion of precontract tender arrangements within the scope of contract review activities

References

❶ Managing Internal Interfaces (T-14)

❷ Design Control (L-2)

Overview

Design control differentiates ISO 9001 from ISO 9002, and addresses the design and development of a product or service. The intent of this element is simply to ensure that user or customer requirements, both stated and implied, are specified and met.

Many organizations do not have comprehensive, formalized procedures for design and development activities, and only minimum guidelines are provided to staff to encourage some consistency in approach. However, these controls are often insufficient to provide a formal and controlled development environment. As such, there is usually little repeatability in practices.

Design and Development Planning ❶

As with all activities that impact quality, design and development activities must be assigned to suitably qualified and experienced staff equipped with appropriate resources to complete the design successfully. Internal requirements such as resources, funding, and technical requirements are often defined in design or development plans for a project or product.

Design and development plans are also the vehicles whereby an organization can tailor a standard design process. If projects are limited in scope or size (not warranting a full-fledged, formalized development process), then development plans cater to deviation from the overall development process. In some respects, design plans are another form of detailed quality plan, and define such details as:

✔ Design input requirements (from contract review activities)

✔ Chosen development methodology (where there is a deviation from the standard design process)

✔ Resources required by the project or program to ensure cross-functional participation (including customers, suppliers, and contractors where appropriate)

✔ Major milestones whereby the project schedule can be tracked

✔ Deliverables across all phases of the development process (e.g., design specifications, functional specifications, test plans, systems integration plans, and acceptance test plans)

✔ Controls or decision gates between these design phases (e.g., customer reviews and first article inspections)

✔ Verification and validation test activities

Design plans are not normally static, and as such, any changes to these plans (including design changes) must be documented and communicated.

Organizational and Technical Interfaces ❷

Another aspect of design planning is the need to define which functions or internal groups need to be involved at the various design stages. For example, if product manufacturability is a key design requirement, the design plans need to ensure that suitably qualified representatives from the manufacturing group receive relevant design records, and that the group participate in design review meetings where appropriate. Development plans are the tools whereby such interfaces are defined, and provide the means of communicating design details and changes between different groups.

Some companies overcome some of the difficulties involved in managing these interfaces through the use of Integrated Product Teams (IPTs). IPTs include representatives from the different engineering disciplines such as mechanical, software, hardware, and systems engineering. These teams also include representatives from other functional groups involved with the product, project, or program, for example, manufacturing, contracts and sales, marketing, program management, and quality assurance.

Design Input ❸

All design requirements (or design inputs) must be identified, documented, and reviewed. ISO 9001 makes reference to contract review activities (4.3) that provide design input in the form of flowdown of customer requirements. Initial reviews of design input are essential in order to resolve any ambiguities or potential misunderstandings and begin with a thorough understanding of customer requirements.

There are many examples of design input, including applicable statutory and regulatory product requirements, requirement specifications, stated and implied needs of the customer or user (usability, reliability, etc.), and internal requirements (e.g., manufacturability, serviceability, design to cost, etc.).

Regardless of their origin (whether they come from an external customer or an internal organization such as a marketing group), user requirements need to be clearly documented and agreed upon by all parties. This will include any requirements that become apparent after the design process has started.

Design Output ❹

All design output must be documented in such a way that it can be both verified against design input requirements and validated. Examples include design specifications, functional specifications, test plans, systems integration plans, and acceptance test plans. As ISO 9001 suggests, design output must:

✔ Meet the specified design input requirements identified at the start of the design process

✔ Contain or make reference to acceptance criteria defined as design input

✔ Identify design characteristics that are important to ensure the safe and proper functioning of the product, for example, characteristics for operation, storage, etc.

Prior to release, design output documents must be reviewed and approved by authorized staff. As with all design records, suitable document control measures are necessary to ensure the currency and accessiblility of records during the design process.

Design Review

Design control requires that formal reviews of the design results are planned and conducted at appropriate intervals (typically defined in design plans). Design reviews will include representatives of all functions concerned with the design stage being reviewed, and in some instances, even the customer. These reviews must be documented or recorded (4.16), usually in the form of design review meeting minutes.

Design Verification

The clause requires that, at appropriate stages of the design process, design verification must be conducted to ensure that the design output from each stage (specifications, plans, etc.) meets the design input for that phase. Results of design verification activities must be documented and maintained.

Design verification activities may include comparing the new design with a similar proven design (if available), reviewing the design-stage documents before release, simulations, and prototypes. Taking prototyping as an example, suitable controls would include identification of prototype versions and traceability of results to a particular design.

It is quite often difficult to distinguish between different stages of design. When migration between design stages is more questionable, it is often helpful to focus on the points of delivery between areas of design responsibility, whether they are individuals or organizations. These may well prove to be useful points of design reviews and verification.

Design Validation

Following successful design verification through the design process, design validation must be performed to ensure that the final design output meets the initial design input. There are instances when, for example, design validation is performed earlier in the design process.

A point of clarification in the 1994 version of the standard is the distinction between "verification" and "validation." One easy way to think of this is with the questions, "Are we building the product right?" (verification) and "Are we building the right product?" (validation). To elaborate, validation determines whether user needs and requirements are met by the final design; verification determines whether the design is being carried out as intended at any given point in the design process.

Validation is broader than verification. It is an all-encompassing formal study to prove that stated objectives can consistently be met. It often involves the customer directly, or indirectly through the use of clinical trials or pre-market testing through marketing focus groups.

Design Changes ❺ ❻

The element requires that all design changes and modifications must be identified, documented, reviewed by the appropriate parties, and approved by authorized staff before their implementation. These changes are typically discussed as a part of design reviews, with the changes themselves managed through configuration management or an Engineering Change Order (ECO) process.

General ❼

The documented design process often does not provide the flexibility needed to allow the designers enough freedom to do their work effectively. Sometimes the culture within an organization will not support the extent or rigor of verification activities and recordkeeping.

It is important to ensure that an appropriate level of flexibility is built into the design process to address this issue, while ensuring that sufficient control is always exercised.

Documentation Required

✔ Procedures, guidelines, and work instructions describing all activities and all stages of the design and development process

✔ Plans and schedules for each project, including the tasks, assignments, validation activities, and verification activities to occur

✔ Design specifications or requirements documents that describe the design in terms traceable to user or customer requirements (stated and implied)

Implementation Approach

✔ Determine what current design activities meet the intent of ISO 9001.

✔ Obtain feedback from design staff regarding the value of what they currently do and identify opportunities for improvement and increased control.

✔ Use this information to agree on and document current design practices in the form of a design and development methodology.

✔ Ensure widespread training in this methodology to facilitate its adoption.

✔ Establish history with the new procedures and records so that the defined development methodology can demonstrate effective implementation.

Changes from ISO 9001 (1987)

✔ Addresses the need for design reviews at appropriate intervals

✔ Clarifies differences between design verification and validation activities

✔ Now specifies that design output documents be reviewed prior to release

✔ Clarifies the differences between design verification and validation activities

References

❶ Quality Planning (M-4)

❷ Organization (M-2)

❸ Contract Review (L-1)

❹ Control of Quality Records (E-3)

❺ Document and Data Control (E-2)

❻ Product Identification and Traceability (S-3)

❼ Process Libraries (T-13)

Overview ❶ ❷ ❸ ❹

Process control refers to the post-design activities of a product or service lifecycle, including production, manufacturing, installation, and servicing. It requires the organization to provide what it terms *controlled* conditions.

It also requires that all production processes affecting quality be documented, in addition to production planning, which is often addressed through quality plans supporting a product or project. Quality plans and procedures should specify materials, processes, equipment, reference standards, and any process capability studies. Such procedures should address any workmanship criteria that are appropriate. Often, models, samples, and illustrations of finished product are provided to the operators for reference.

The clause states that all production, installation, and servicing equipment must be addressed within the quality management system (BMS), in terms of:

✔ Equipment approval (where appropriate)
✔ Use of production equipment (procedures and operating instructions)
✔ Providing a suitable working environment (including safety issues)

The standard stresses the importance of addressing any training requirements (4.18) necessary for process and equipment operators, demonstrating the suitability of their experience and qualifications. The same principles apply to service organizations, where the staff delivering the service need to be able to demonstrate the appropriate training and experience.

ISO 9001 (1994) now specifies that equipment maintenance must be addressed to help ensure that process capability and consistency is maintained. This will involve regular calibration of equipment addressed elsewhere in ISO 9001 (4.11). In addition to restating the need for processes to be controlled and documented, the clause also requires that production processes be monitored and controlled in terms of suitable process parameters and product characteristics (such as acceptance criteria).

The ISO 9000 series makes reference to so-called *special processes* whose results cannot be fully verified by subsequent inspection and testing of the product. In such instances, process deficiencies or nonconformities may become apparent only after the product has been shipped to the customer or in use. Verification activities associated with such processes must be performed by qualified operators who can demonstrate suitable skills, knowledge, experience, and qualifications. Examples of special processes include:

✔ Soldering
✔ Some production processes in the chemical industry
✔ Food production
✔ Some software applications

Special processes typically require continuous process monitoring to ensure that specified design requirements continue to be met.

As with all processes within the management system, comprehensive quality records should be maintained addressing processes, equipment, and staff or operator training.

Documentation Required

✔ Documented processes addressing all aspects of production, installation, and servicing activities relating to the product or service delivery

✔ Work instructions, including instructions on equipment use

Implementation Approach

✔ Review current processes for compliance, conducting process capability studies wherever appropriate.

✔ Identify any special processes.

✔ Define and document production, installation, and servicing processes.

✔ Verify the training and experience of staff and operators.

Changes from ISO 9001 (1987)

✔ Now addresses servicing processes (previously a separate subclause)

✔ Need for equipment maintenance stated, including calibration

References

❶ Quality Planning (M-4)

❷ Training (E-4)

❸ Control of Quality Records (E-3)

❹ Control of Inspection, Measuring, and Test Equipment (S-5)

Overview ❶ ❷

This element requires that adequate controls are exercised over the product in the following respects: handling, storage, packaging, preservation, and delivery. The purpose of the element is to ensure that product reaching the customer is in a condition consistent with stated and implied needs. These requirements apply to the product while it is under the contractual responsibility of the supplier.

Suitable handling requirements may apply at all stages of development, production, and post-production activities, so as to prevent damage or deterioration of the product. For example, electronic components can be affected by electrostatic discharge (ESD) when the operator is not sufficiently equipped with antistatic measures, such as wrist or heel straps.

Provision for storage should address any factors that may cause a product to deteriorate over time or become damaged when insufficient controls are exercised. Any stock rotation practices should be addressed, particularly where periodic examination of the products is required to ensure preservation. Where appropriate, perishable products or products with limited shelf life should be marked with allocated expiration dates.

Needless to say, any labels or stickers attached to products in storage should remain legible and not deteriorate over time. When products must be stored within certain temperature and humidity ranges, suitable measurements should be taken periodically to verify that the environmental conditions are proper to ensure that the product is not damaged in any way.

In the case of product packaging, it is important to consider whether the packaging is appropriate to prevent damage to the product and to clearly identify what the packaging contains.

Many of the above issues apply to the delivery of the product to the customer, where it is contractually specified. When the delivery of product is outsourced to subcontractors or third parties, suitable vendor control must be exercised in the purchasing process.

It is worth stressing that the scope of this element of ISO 9001 covers the majority of design, production, purchasing, installation, and servicing activities.

For example, handling requirements are required from the receipt of materials prior to production, through installation of a product at a customer site. Storage requirements impact receiving materials and finished product ready for delivery, and so on.

Documentation Required

✔ Documented procedures addressing the handling, storage, packaging, preservation, and delivery of products and materials

Implementation Approach

✔ Review current practice and identify any shortcomings in control.

✔ Produce procedures addressing these issues throughout the product or service lifecycle.

Changes from ISO 9001 (1987)

✔ Addresses the need for controls to ensure the preservation of products

✔ Now clarifies the need for *designated* (rather than *secure*) storage areas

References

❶ Purchasing (S-1)

❷ Inspection and Testing (S-4)

Overview ❶ ❷

This clause was previously found only in ISO 9001, but with the 1994 revision of the standards, it can now also be found in ISO 9002. It relates to the servicing and maintenance activities supporting a product or service after it has been delivered to the customer.

Just as the product must be produced and developed under controlled quality conditions, the same applies to servicing or maintenance where it is often a specified part of the contract with the customer. ISO 9001 suggests that service reports are an example of the need for the controls exercised over servicing to be integrated within the overall management system (4.14.3, Preventive Action).

There are many examples of how servicing is provided to customers, including:

✔ Spare parts or the supply of new parts
✔ Customer technical support, advice, and post-sales support
✔ Equipment installation, maintenance, and servicing
✔ Other types of product support such as product repair

Servicing requires the same type of controls as product development and manufacture. Suitably trained service staff must be provided to conduct servicing activities, with appropriate technical and product experience. Any servicing equipment must be controlled and calibrated to ensure its continued accuracy, and all activities must be defined and documented in servicing procedures.

Some servicing activities may be provided by an external party or subcontractor. In this instance, suitable controls must be exercised, and the usual subcontractor selection and management process applied. All instances of servicing must be addressed in contract review activities to clarify servicing or maintenance responsibilities of both the supplier and the customer.

Documentation Required

✔ Documented procedures addressing servicing and maintenance activities, including detailed work instructions for any field personnel
✔ Suitable product documentation available to customers

Implementation Approach

✔ Review current processes and formalize the practices.
✔ Ensure that servicing activities interface effectively with other parts of the management system.
✔ Provide suitable training and resources to field staff.

References

❶ Control of Customer-Supplied Product (S-2)
❷ Corrective and Preventive Action (C-1)

Contract Review (4.3)

How are contracts currently documented, reviewed, and approved?

Is provision made in contracts for changes or amendments? Is this process for managing and communicating contract changes defined?

What types of verification activity is performed on contracts to ensure that the contract can be honored?

How are internal customer/supplier relationships managed?

Design Control (4.4)

What is an appropriate level of minimum control in the design process?

Is design and development planning being carried out?

How formal are the design reviews and what records are kept?

Does the same level of control occur for various scales of projects?

What types of design output exist?

How will any changes in design or user requirements be controlled during development?

Process Control (4.9)

What production planning is performed?

How are production, installation, and processes approved?

What skills are required by staff and operating personnel?

Is production equipment suitably controlled and maintained?

What kind of process capability studies are performed?

Do production processes include any such special processes?

Handling, Storage, Packaging, and Delivery (4.15)

Are suitable controls being exercised over the product to ensure that it is not inadvertently damaged?

In the case of subcontractors providing packaging or delivery services, is the subcontractor fully aware of the requirements of the products?

Servicing (4.19)

What installation, post-sales support, servicing or maintenance services are provided to customers?

How is servicing data fed back into the management system through the corrective and preventive action systems?

What contract review activities are performed regarding servicing?

ISO 9000
Management Systems

Support
Activities

Purchasing, 4.6 (S-1)
Control of Customer-Supplied Product, 4.7 (S-2)
Product Identification and Traceability, 4.8 (S-3)
Inspection and Testing, 4.10 (S-4)
Control of Inspection, Measuring, and Test Equipment, 4.11 (S-5)
Inspection and Test Status, 4.12 (S-6)

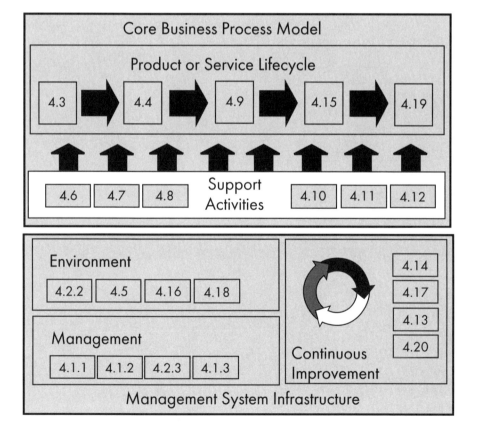

Overview ❶ ❷ ❸ ❹

This clause addresses the requirements for an organization in the areas of purchasing activities and the management of suppliers. ISO 9001 uses the term *subcontractor* to apply to both product and material suppliers as well as subcontractors providing services. Examples of service providers include financial auditors, consulting firms, registrars, external development companies or production organizations, and any *outsourced* functions. With the trend toward outsourcing activities to other external partners (sometimes even within an organization), management of these interfaces with suppliers is equally important to managing more traditional suppliers. Historically, most companies have instead relied on costly receiving inspection to verify the quality of parts.

The main requirements of this element are that a supplier establish documented purchasing and supplier management processes (Figure S-1), and maintain an **approved supplier list** (ASL) or **approved vendor list** (AVL) that list all suppliers (product and service) and their approval status.

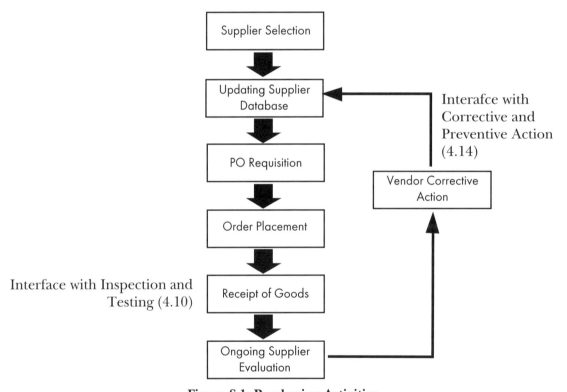

Figure S-1: Purchasing Activities

Some suppliers will lose their *approved supplier status* if quality problems are identified and not adequately addressed. The basis for selecting a new supplier and adding it to the ASL should be defined. Typically, the selection criteria will include quality, delivery, service, and cost. They may be judged on the basis of past experience, quality system requirements, second-party audits, or product evaluations. In some cases, only a single source may exist.

Often, an organization will use integrated financial or business software that includes accounts payable, accounts receivable, and an ASL in one application. In this instance, and when a computer printout is maintained for reference, this list must be identified in order to illustrate its validity (because such a list is potentially inaccurate as soon as it is printed if a supplier is either added or deleted). In the case of doubt, the on-line ASL should be viewed.

It is important to define the type and extent of control exercised over suppliers (e.g., supplier quality audits), and this is dependent on a risk assessment associated with the impact a supplier may have on overall product or service quality. Many companies divide their suppliers into different categories, such as *key suppliers*.

In order to ensure that purchased product conforms to specified requirements, the clause requires that suitable and comprehensive purchasing data (such as technical specifications) be provided to the supplier to avoid misunderstanding and the delivery of unsuitable products. Purchasing data may make reference to such information as product characteristics, national standards, or testing methods.

The clause also addresses two scenarios under which verification activities must be addressed, where appropriate. The scenarios are as follows:

✔ When an organization may wish to verify purchased product at the supplier's premises
✔ When a customer may wish to verify product at the supplier's premises. (The standard is clear that this does not absolve the organization of responsibility for ensuring that quality requirements have been met.)

Documentation Required

✔ Documented processes addressing all purchasing activities and any verification activities such as second-party audits
✔ An approved vendor list (AVL)

Implementation Approach

✔ Review current practice and identify any shortcomings.
✔ Create procedures and work instructions defining purchasing activities.

Changes from ISO 9001 (1987)

✔ Addition of clause addressing supplier verification at subcontractor's premises

References

❶ Designing the BMS Infrastructure (T-10)
❷ Inspection and Testing (S-4)
❸ Corrective and Preventive Action (C-1)
❹ Control of Customer-Supplied Product (S-2)

Overview ❶ ❷ ❸ ❹

Customer-supplied product is product (or service) supplied (or provided) by the customer for use or incorporation during the design, production, or assembly into the final product, or maintenance of the product.

Such products are found at the companies' sites and, since they fall under the scope of the management system, must be adequately controlled and managed. There are many examples of customer-supplied product, including:

✔ Product returns, either for repair or servicing
✔ Software or hardware provided for incorporation into the end product or system
✔ Customer-provided collection of end product
✔ Customer-provided plant and equipment for manufacturing processes
✔ Customer-provided test stations

Activities for the receiving, verifying, storing, and maintenance of these products will need to be defined. In the case of damage to the customer-supplied product or unsuitability for its intended use, the customer must be notified and the issue resolved to the satisfaction of both the supplier and the customer.

Documentation Required

✔ Documented processes addressing the control of customer-supplied products

Implementation Approach

✔ List all customer-supplied products or services.
✔ Define and document how these products are managed and controlled on site.

Changes from ISO 9001 (1987)

✔ Addition of a caveat regarding verification activities and a supplier's responsibility to provide only acceptable product that conforms to specified requirements

References

❶ Servicing (L-5)
❷ Handling, Storage, Packaging, Preservation, and Delivery (L-4)
❸ Process Control (L-3)
❹ Corrective and Preventive Action (C-1)

Overview ❶ ❷ ❸

This clause of the standard requires an organization to define and document how it provides product traceability through the entire product lifecycle: development, production, installation, servicing, and maintenance. It is written with enough flexibility to allow a company to determine what level of traceability is appropriate to the product. At the same time, a minimum level of traceability is often required by regulatory or customer requirements.

Traceability helps to ensure that product or material issues can be traced back to an earlier design or production process, or even the supplier for evaluation of the cause for nonconformance. In extreme cases, traceability is essential for recalling any defective products from the marketplace or field.

The degree of traceability will require one or more of the following factors:

✔ Customer or contractual requirements
✔ Industry regulations
✔ Industry-accepted best practice

In all these cases, the level of traceability will be dependent on the supplier performing a risk assessment and determining the appropriate level of control. Typically, the types of traceability performed range from no traceability, individual product unit or component traceability, to batch or lot traceability, depending on the nature of the product. Some industries, such as the defense and space industries, require 100 percent traceability. Comparing current practice with that of similar companies through benchmarking can help determine normal industry practice.

Traceability of a product is usually identified through the use of marks or stickers, serial numbers, or documentation accompanying a product. Often companies use software packages that automate traceability and configuration management.

Documentation Required

✔ Documented processes addressing what level of traceability is required and how traceability of product is maintained at all stages throughout the product lifecycle

Implementation Approach

✔ Agree upon appropriate levels of traceability by using a risk assessment or comparing practices with industry leaders as appropriate.
✔ Define and document procedures addressing traceability control.

References

❶ Contract Review (L-1)
❷ Inspection and Test Status (S-6)
❸ Document and Data Control (E-2)

Overview ❶ ❷ ❸ ❹ ❺ ❻

This clause addresses the need for a company to have quality plans and documented procedures for the inspection and testing of product or service at appropriate stages in its lifecycle. Specifically, ISO 9001 addresses the need for the following testing and inspection:

✔ Receiving inspection when product or material is received from a supplier

✔ In-process inspection during development and production phases

✔ Final inspection and test before installation or delivery to a customer

Receiving inspection and testing of product are required to help ensure that incoming product is not used or processed in any way until it has been inspected or otherwise verified as conforming to specific requirements as defined by the purchasing process. The degree and nature of receiving inspection should take into account the amount of control exercised at the supplier's premises, as detailed in any inspection or test documentation accompanying the product or materials. Many companies operate a materials review board (MRB) to oversee quality assurance and quality control activities over incoming materials.

ISO 9001 allows for the scenario where, for urgent production purposes, full verification that product conforms to requirements may not be possible. In this case, such product must be identified and recorded to allow for immediate traceability and recall for replacement in the event that it is nonconforming.

In-process inspection and testing refers to the need for testing during the development and production processes. It requires the organization to hold product until the necessary inspection and tests have been conducted, or the inspection and test records have been received and verified.

Final inspection and testing provide the final confidence and evidence that the product characteristics conform to specified requirements. The quality plan and documented procedures for final inspection and testing specify all inspections that must be performed. No product should be dispatched either to the customer or to storage pending delivery until all the inspection and test activities have been completed, and the inspection or test records are authorized by the staff responsible for the release of product.

At all stages in the lifecycle, it is necessary to maintain full records to demonstrate that the product has been inspected and tested according to the procedures or quality plan associated with that product. Should the product fail to pass any inspection or testing required of it, the procedures for control of nonconforming product should be applied.

Documentation Required

✔ Documented processes addressing the inspection and test practices for product and materials at all stages of the product lifecycle

✔ Detailed inspection and test requirements specified in the product or service quality plan (or equivalent)

Implementation Approach

✔ Review current practices for inspection and testing of product throughout the lifecycle, comparing the requirements of ISO 9001 against existing processes.

✔ Define and document procedures and instructions covering inspection and testing activities.

✔ Consider the interfaces with the other support activities such as Inspection and Test Status (4.12).

Changes from ISO 9001 (1987)

✔ Consideration is given to the level of testing and inspection of product or service provided by the supplier.

✔ Addresses the need for suitable controls when product is urgently released for production.

✔ References the need for failed product to initiate procedures for the control of nonconforming product.

References

❶ Control of Inspection, Measuring, and Test Equipment (S-5)

❷ Inspection and Test Status (S-6)

❸ Control of Nonconforming Product (C-3)

❹ Process Control (L-3)

❺ Purchasing (S-1)

❻ Product Identification and Traceability (S-3)

Overview ❶ ❷ ❸ ❹

This clause of the standard requires that a company maintain documented procedures addressing the control, calibration, and maintenance of all equipment used to demonstrate the product's conformance to specified requirements. Such equipment includes:

✔ Inspection equipment
✔ Measuring equipment and devices
✔ Test equipment (including test software and hardware)

The purpose of this element is to ensure that equipment is used in a manner that ensures that the measurement uncertainty is known and consistent with the required product characteristics. It applies not only to production processes, but also to equipment used in installation and servicing, and even that used during development.

It does not require that all equipment within an organization be calibrated, only the equipment affecting quality or verifying conformance to specified requirements. All such equipment must be capable of providing the necessary accuracy and precision (*acceptance criteria* or *tolerance limits*).

A calibration program with supporting procedures must be established and maintained for all equipment used to verify product conformance. For each item of equipment, this program must address:

✔ Details of equipment type, unique identification and location, calibration method, acceptance criteria, acceptable operating ranges
✔ Calibration frequency and details of the checks to be performed
✔ Actions to be taken when calibration results are outside of operating parameters (including the need in this instance to assess the validity of previous inspection and test results)
✔ Identifier or approved record or marks to show the calibration status
✔ Availability of technical data to the customer in order to verify that the equipment is functioning within acceptable ranges

The frequency and nature of equipment calibration must reference one or more of the following factors (listed in preferred order):

1. Recognized national or international standards
2. Equipment manufacturer's recommendations
3. Certified equipment known to operate within acceptable ranges
4. Company documented requirements or standards (in the absence of the above)

Where no such controls exist, a risk assessment should be performed and recorded to assess such factors as the role of the equipment, frequency of use, required tolerance limits, and the use of the data from the equipment in supporting a product specification.

Most companies outsource calibration activities, usually to a test house certified with the National Institute of Standards and Technology (NIST). These accredited test houses help log the calibration program for equipment, advising a company when equipment requires calibration. In the case of a test house or laboratory, it may be possible for an organization to calibrate an appropriate amount of equipment externally, and then use this equipment as the baseline for calibrating the remaining equipment internally.

To help ensure that equipment remains within acceptable tolerance limits, the standard requires that the work environment (temperature, humidity, etc.) be suitably controlled, and that all equipment is properly handled and stored (4.15).

Full calibration records must be maintained. Many organizations maintain a calibration log to record the status of inspection, testing, and measuring equipment (4.16).

Documentation Required

✔ Full procedure set addressing the maintenance of a calibration program
✔ Calibration log addressing all equipment under the calibration program

Implementation Approach

✔ Review current procedures and practices for adequacy, and identify shortcomings.
✔ Identify all equipment that must be calibrated.
✔ Produce a calibration log capturing all relevant information for each item of inspection, measuring, and testing equipment.
✔ Introduce procedures and work instructions for maintaining a calibration program.

References

❶ Inspection and Testing (S-4)
❷ Control of Quality Records (E-3)
❸ Process Control (L-3)
❹ Handling, Storage, Packaging, Preservation, and Delivery (L-4)

Overview ❶ ❷

This element of the standard requires that all products demonstrate their test or inspection status through the production processes including, where appropriate, installation, and servicing. The objective of the requirement is to avoid the inadvertent use or delivery of nonconforming product to the customer. The exception to the rule concerns products that have failed certain testing or inspection requirements, but are allowed under an authorized concession. Only products that have passed all the necessary inspections and tests are delivered to customers.

There are many ways to demonstrate inspection and test status, including:

✔ Stamps, tags, stickers, or inspection records that accompany the product through the production processes

✔ Use of serial numbers, bar codes, and database tracking systems to automate the tracking and labeling processes

✔ Segregation and quarantining of nonconforming products

Documentation Required

✔ Documented processes addressing the labeling, segregation, or other means whereby product status can be identified through production, installation, and servicing

✔ Records to show product status at all stages of the product or service lifecycle

Implementation Approach

✔ Review current means of identifying product status.

✔ Define requirements for addressing inspection and test status.

✔ Define requirements for concessions and waivers for nonconforming product.

Changes from ISO 9001 (1987)

✔ References authorized concessions in disposition of products that have failed inspection and testing

References

❶ Product Identification and Traceability (S-3)

❷ Control of Nonconforming Product (C-3)

Purchasing (S-1)

What is the criteria used to select suppliers and subcontractors?

Is an approved list of such suppliers maintained?

What information is required on purchase orders?

Do contracts sometimes allow customer verification activities?

How is the performance of suppliers measured?

Control of Customer-Supplied Product (S-2)

What customer-supplied products can be found within the organization?

How are these products currently controlled?

How are problems with these products resolved?

Product Identification and Traceability (S-3)

What degree of traceability is appropriate to customer needs and expectations?

Are there industry regulations governing the level of traceability required?

How can traceability be identified on the product?

Inspection and Testing (S-4)

What level of receiving inspection is appropriate considering the testing conducted by the supplier prior to receipt?

What controls exist for urgently required production materials?

At what stages through the production process should products and materials be inspected and/or tested?

What inspection and test processes are required during development?

What happens to product that fails inspection and/or testing?

Control of Inspection, Measuring, and Test Equipment (S-5)

Which equipment affects quality or verifies product conformance?

What are the appropriate methods and frequency of checks required?

How is the calibration of equipment identified?

Who is responsible for ensuring that equipment is calibrated and operating within acceptable tolerance limits?

Is the work environment monitored to ensure that equipment is not being inadvertently damaged?

Inspection and Test Status (S-6)

How is the product's status currently demonstrated?

Is inspection status maintained through the production process?

At what stages during development and production is test status most critical?

Glossary

Accreditation
The process or procedure whereby an accreditation agency recognizes a registrar as competent to offer independent assessment services against national and international standards, including the ISO 9000 series.

Audit
A planned, independent, and documented assessment of an organization or function to determine whether quality objectives and other conformance requirements are being met.

Auditee
An organization or individual subject to an audit.

Author
The individual responsible for creating and maintaining a document.

Business Management System
The integrated business and quality management system providing an optimal working environment to support an organization's quality and business objectives.

Calibration
The procedure or process whereby inspection, measuring, and testing equipment is verified as operating within accepted tolerance limits.

Certification
The process whereby a third party gives written assurance that a product, process, or service conforms to specified requirements.

Compliance
An indication or judgment based on objective evidence that the supplier of a product or service has met the requirements of the relevant specifications, contract, or regulation.

Conformance
An indication or judgment based on objective evidence that a product or service has met the requirements of the relevant specifications, contract, or regulation.

Contractor
An organization that provides a product or service to a customer in a contractual situation.

Corrective Action
Action taken to eliminate the causes of an existing nonconformance, defect, or other undesirable situation in order to prevent its recurrence.

Customer
Ultimate consumer, user, client, beneficiary, or second party.

Finding
A conclusion of importance based on observation(s).

Inspection

Activities such as measuring, examining, testing, or gauging one or more characteristics of a product or service, and comparing these with specified requirements to determine conformity.

Nonconformity

The nonfulfillment of a specified requirement.

Notified Body

A third-party organization, designated by a competent authority to carry out conformity assessment procedures specified in European Union (EU) directives.

Owner

The individual assigned responsibility and authority for a process, system, area, or document.

Preventive Action

Action taken to eliminate the causes of a potential nonconformance, defect, or other undesirable situation in order to prevent its occurrence.

Process

A set of interrelated resources and activities that transforms inputs into outputs.

Purchaser

The recipient of a product or service provided by the supplier in a contractual situation.

Quality

The totality of features and characteristics of a product or process that bear on its ability to satisfy stated or implied needs.

Quality Assurance

All the planned and systematic activities implemented within the quality system and demonstrated as needed to provide adequate confidence that an organization will fulfill requirements for quality.

Quality Control

The operational techniques and activities that are used to fulfill requirements for quality.

Quality Management

That aspect of the overall management function that determines and implements the quality policy.

Quality Management System

The management system addressing management control, organization structure, process management, continuous improvement, and resources and responsibilities in support of the organization's quality and business objectives.

Quality Plan

A document stating the specific quality practices, resources, and sequence of activities relevant to a particular product, project, process, or contract.

Quality Policy

The overall quality intentions and direction of an organization regarding quality, as formally expressed by top management.

Quality System

The organizational structure, responsibilities, procedures, processes, and resources for implementing quality management.

Registrar

The accredited third party that assesses a supplier's quality management system and, if it conforms with specified requirements, grants registration to the supplier (also known in Europe as a certification body).

Registration

Process by which a recognized third party indicates relevant characteristics of a product, process, or service, and then includes or registers the product, process, or service in an appropriate publicly available list.

Subcontractor

A supplier of services to an organization in a contractual situation.

Supplier

An organization that provides a product or a service to a customer in a contractual situation.

Technical Expert

A member of staff with expertise relating to an individual process.

Traceability

The ability to trace the history, application, or location of a product by means of recorded identifications.

Validation

The process of evaluating a product or service to ensure compliance with specified requirements.

Verification

The act of reviewing, inspecting, testing, checking, auditing, or otherwise establishing and documenting whether products, processes, services, or documents conform to specified requirements.

The definitions contained within this glossary are compiled from various sources, including ISO 8402 (Quality Vocabulary) and ISO/IEC Guide 2. They are intended to be *working* definitions in the context of this Manual, however, and have been amended to add clarity.

Bibliography

A number of national and international standards have been used in compiling the Manual. These standards are listed below.

ISO 9001 (1994)
Quality systems–Model for quality assurance in design/development, production, installation, and servicing

ISO 9002 (1994)
Quality systems–Model for quality assurance in production, installation, and servicing

ISO 9003 (1994)
Quality systems–Model for quality assurance in final inspection and testing

ISO 9000-1 (1994)
Quality management and quality assurance–Guidelines for selection and use

ISO 9004-1 (1994)
Quality management and quality system elements–Guidelines

ISO 8402 (1986)
Quality–Vocabulary

BS 6143 Part 2 (1990)
Guide to the economics of quality

ISO 10011 Parts 1 to 3 (1993)
Guidelines for auditing quality systems

ISO 10013 (1993)
Guidelines for developing quality manuals

ISO 9000-3 (1991)
Guide to the application of ISO 9001 to the development, supply, and maintenance of software

ISO 9004-2 (1991)
Guide to quality management and quality system elements for services

BS 4891 (1972)
A guide to quality assurance

BS 7850 1&2 (1992)
Total quality management

ISO 9000-4 (1993)
Quality systems: Guide to dependability programme management

XIS Consulting, Inc.

The author of this Manual, James Davies, is a founding principal of XIS Consulting, Inc., which specializes in process improvement and quality management initiatives and provides a wide range of consulting and training services across all industries.

For further information on the consulting and training services supporting the material in this Manual, please contact:

James Davies
XIS Consulting, Inc.
5714 Folsom Boulevard
Suite 164
Sacramento, CA 95819-4608

Tel: 800-947-0040
Fax: 916-739-8768
email: james@xisinc.com
        www.xisinc.com

User Registration

Name: _____

Title: _____
Company: _____
Address: _____
City/State _____ ZIP: _____
Tel: _____
Fax: _____
Email: _____

Registering this Manual with XIS Consulting, Inc. will ensure that you are informed of regular updates and additions (factsheets are regularly reviewed for accuracy, and technical information and concepts updated).

Improvement Suggestion

Factsheet: _____
Description: _____
_____
_____
_____
_____
_____

Attach additional sheets as appropriate.

Please copy, complete, and return by fax to:

James S. Davies
XIS Consulting, Inc.
5714 Folsom Boulevard
Suite 164
Sacramento, CA 95819.4608

Tel: 800-947-0040
Fax: 916-739-8768
email: manual@xisinc.com
         www.xisinc.com

Index

Note: *See also* Glossary, starting on page 205, for defined terms.

Index

Dutch Council for Accreditation (RvA), 16

Environment, 121-130
  defined, 7, 9
  in BMS Infrastructure, 17
  organization, 92-94
  study of, in project approach, 45, 46
External factors, and process libraries, 105

Factsheets, understanding, xii
Flowcharting applications, 82-83
Forms, in BMS infrastructure, 100

Generic guidance on application of ISO 9000, 20
Guide, elements of, 102
Guidelines for Developing Quality Manuals, 9

Handling, storage, packaging, preservation, and delivery, 181-182

Implementation approach:
  for contract review, 173
  for control of inspection, measuring, and test equipment, 197
  for control of nonconforming product, 163
  for control of quality records, 128
  for corrective and preventive action, 158
  for design control, 177
  for document and data control, 125
  for handling, storage, packaging, preservation, and delivery, 182
  for inspection and testing, 195
  for inspection and test status, 198
  for internal quality audits, 162
  for management representative, 140
  for management review, 146
  for organization, 139
  for process control, 180
  for product identification and traceability, 193
  for purchasing, 192
  for quality planning, 143
  for quality policy, 137
  for quality system, 123
  for servicing, 183
  for statistical techniques, 166
  for training, 130
Implementation, of quality system, 123
Initial assessment, in project approach, 53, 55, 73
Inspection and testing, 194-195
Installation, and Servicing, 2
Instructions:
  elements of, 103
  role of, in management system, 122
Integrated Product Teams (IPTs), 175

Internal factors, and process libraries, 105
Internal quality audit, 159-162
  in project approach, 53, 54
Internal interfaces, 109-111
International Organization for Standardization (ISO), 6
Invitation to tender (ITT), defined, 74
IPTs, *see* Integrated product teams
ISO 10011 (1993), 21, 209
ISO 10013 (1993), 22, 209
ISO 6143 Part 2 (1990), 209
ISO 8402 (1986), 209
ISO 9000:
  adoption of, 13
    in United States, 15
    in United Kingdom, 16
  benefits of, 6, 14
  categories of, 19
  conformance standards, 19
  environment of, 14, 15
  as framework for management system, 2
  generic guidance on application of, 20
  industry-specific guidance on application of, 21
  limited scope of, 3
  requirements of, 13
  source of, 6, 13
  terminology, 14
ISO 9000 Business Management System, 7
ISO 9000-1 (1994), 20, 209
ISO 9000-3 (1991), 21, 209
ISO 9000-4 (1991), 21, 209
ISO 9001, 19, 209
  changes from, 123, 125, 128, 137, 139, 146, 158, 162, 166, 177, 180, 182, 191, 192, 195, 198,
  compared to ISO 9002, xiii, 2
  as conformance standard, 19
  generic guidance on application, 20
  industry-specific guidance on application of, 21
ISO 9002, 20, 209
  compared to ISO 9001, xiii, 2
  as conformance standard, 19
  generic guidance on application, 20
ISO 9003, 20, 209
  as conformance standard, 19
  generic guidance on application, 20
ISO 9004-1 (1994), 21, 209
ISO 9004-2 (1991), 209
ITT, *see* Invitation to tender

Key suppliers, 191

Learning organization, defined, 94

Index

Index

About the author

James Davies is a founding principal of XIS Consulting, Inc., a consulting and training company that has worked extensively with Fortune 500 companies with quality management and process improvement initiatives. Prior to this, James was a management consultant with KPMG Peat Marwick LLP and helped establish the West Coast Quality Management Services consulting practice, providing consulting support to a wide variety of quality management projects. James has also worked with the British Standards Institution Quality Assurance (BSI QA), one of the world's leading registrars, where his responsibilities included developing ISO 9000 in the high technology industries in Europe and North America.